Non-verbal Reasoning

Assessment Practice for the 11+

Ages 6–7 Year 2

Alison Primrose

OXFORD
UNIVERSITY PRESS

Great Clarendon Street, Oxford, OX2 6DP, United Kingdom

Oxford University Press is a department of the University of Oxford.
It furthers the University's objective of excellence in research, scholarship,
and education by publishing worldwide. Oxford is a registered trade mark
of Oxford University Press in the UK and in certain other countries

© Oxford University Press 2025
Written by Alison Primrose
Illustrations © Oxford University Press 2025

The moral rights of the author have been asserted
Database right Oxford University Press (maker)

First published in 2025

All rights reserved. No part of this publication may be reproduced,
stored in a retrieval system, transmitted, used for text and data mining,
or used for training artificial intelligence, in any form or by any means,
without the prior permission in writing of Oxford University Press,
or as expressly permitted by law, or under terms agreed with the
appropriate reprographics rights organization. Enquiries concerning
reproduction outside the scope of the above should be sent to the
Rights Department, Oxford University Press, at the address above.

You must not circulate this book in any other binding or cover
and you must impose this same condition on any acquirer

British Library Cataloguing in Publication Data
Data available

978-1-38-206088-2

10 9 8 7 6 5 4 3 2 1

Printed in China

The manufacturing process conforms to the environmental
regulations of the country of origin

Acknowledgements

Content Development Editor and Reviewer: Sue Rowe
Page make-up: York Publishing Solutions Pvt. Ltd.
Cover illustrations: Lo Cole
Illustrations: Nigel Kitching and York Publishing Solutions Pvt. Ltd.

Although we have made every effort to trace and contact
all copyright holders before publication this has not been
possible in all cases. If notified, the publisher will rectify
any errors or omissions at the earliest opportunity.

A Brief History of Bond

Bond 11+ has been the market leader in selective school admission test preparation since 1964, when J.M. Bond published her first book of practice tests.

Jean Moyra Bond was a school principal and passionate educator who started writing out practice questions for her pupils on slips of paper, to help get them test-ready, at a time when no formal resources were available. Her high-quality questions spawned a series of books and the Bond range grew from there; however their original author was advised to publish under her initials, rather than her name, as it was felt that the books would not sell as well if it was known they were written by a woman.

Happily, times have changed; but Jean Moyra Bond's legacy lives on, supporting thousands of pupils on their 11+ journey every year. 'J.M.' Bond was involved in writing and revising Bond materials up until her death in 2011, with the baton being passed on to the new generations of expert tutors who create Bond's peerless learning and practice content.

Now offering cutting-edge digital solutions, as well as a comprehensive print range, Bond remains as the gold standard in 11+ preparation to this day.

Contents

Welcome 4
A Note for Parents 4
How to Use This Book 5
Non-verbal Reasoning Skills 7

Learning Papers

1 Odd One Out 8
2 Series 13
3 Similarities 20
4 Missing Pieces 25
5 Analogies 32
6 Hidden Shape 39
7 Matching Shapes or Reflections 43
8 Combining Shapes 48
Puzzle 1 52

Mixed Papers

Mixed Paper 1 53
Mixed Paper 2 58
Mixed Paper 3 63
Mixed Paper 4 68
Mixed Paper 5 72
Mixed Paper 6 77
Mixed Paper 7 81
Mixed Paper 8 86
Puzzle 2 91

Keywords 92
Answers A1
Progress Chart A10

Welcome

Bond's non-verbal reasoning resources provide thorough and continuous practice for key non-verbal reasoning skills. They are ideal preparation for the **11+ and other selective school entrance exams.**

Bond offers a complete, flexible programme of preparation materials that you can adapt to your child's specific needs. We provide a wide selection of question types and believes that an enriched education is the best preparation. We help children to both master the techniques and develop the logic and rationale to tackle any unknown question types.

KEY STUDY SKILLS

Here are some tips to help:

- Balance short bursts of practice with longer assessment papers.
- Create a quiet study space with pencils, an eraser and paper for working out.
- Limit distractions such as television, technology and games.
- Remember that errors are useful – they are part of the journey to success.

A Note for Parents

Parents have a crucial role in helping children and motivating them. Here are some ways that you can really make a difference.

- Check your child is working at the right level. The goal is being able to score 85% on average. It is demotivating if they cannot complete questions.

- Mark work promptly and go through errors. If papers have not been marked, a child has no idea how they are doing or whether they are repeating the same mistakes.

- Limit the range of homework you give your child. The best results are achieved by a system that gradually increases in difficulty. Completing lots of books and papers does not guarantee your child's success and often creates stress.

- If your child is struggling with something specific, add additional support in that area.

- Communication is key. Encourage your child to focus on the positive.

How to Use This Book

It is very important you find the time to work through this book with your child. It is likely they will need support to understand the Key Skill explanations. Once these elements are understood the questions should be more easily accessed by them independently.

This book includes many step-by-step techniques for solving different question types.

- The first section of the book is the Learning Papers that focus on key skills with worked examples then questions for consolidation.
- The second section of the book is Mixed Papers so that children continue to consolidate and do not forget what they have learnt.
- There are fully worked out answers to explain how an answer has been reached.

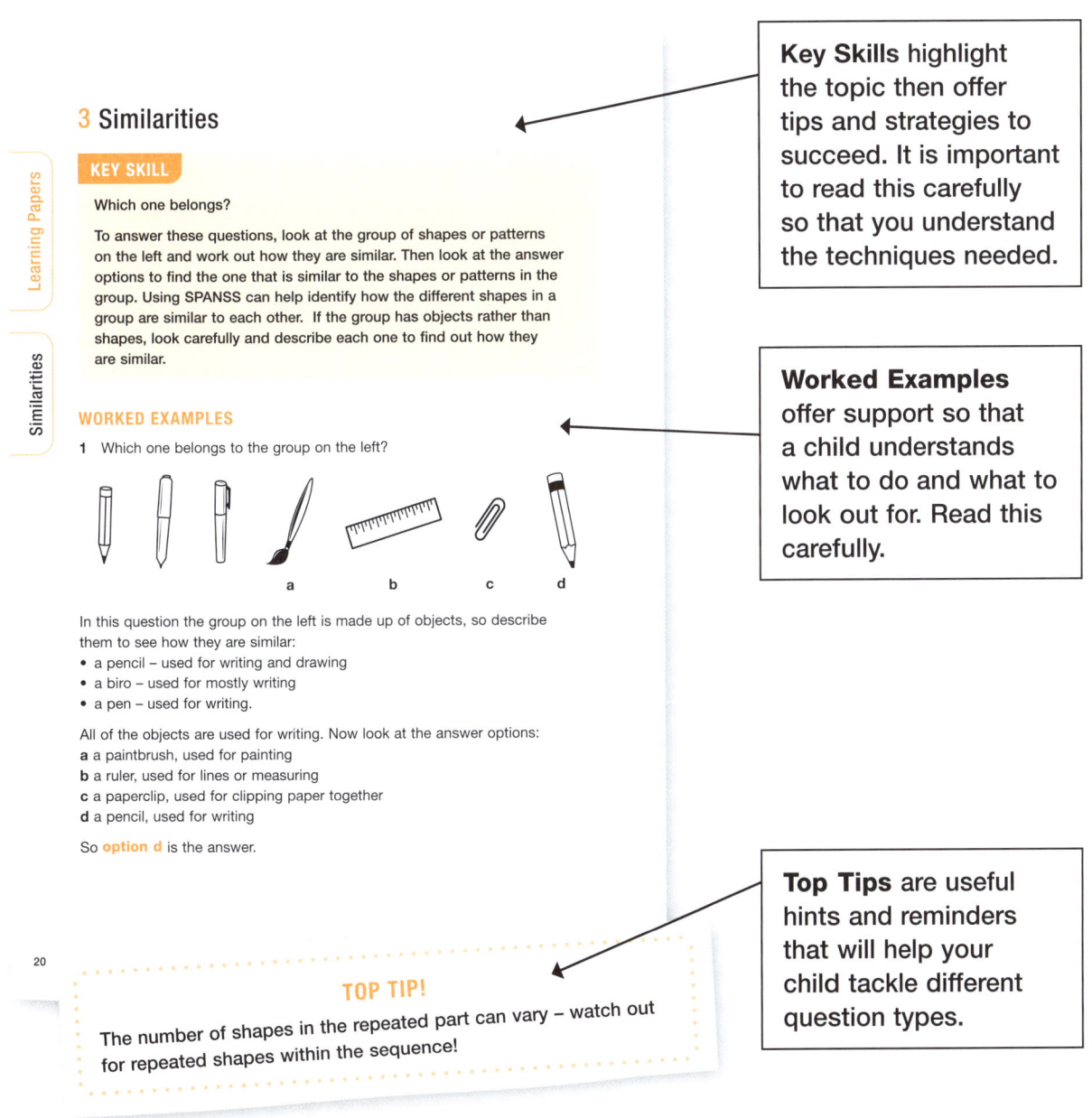

Key Skills highlight the topic then offer tips and strategies to succeed. It is important to read this carefully so that you understand the techniques needed.

Worked Examples offer support so that a child understands what to do and what to look out for. Read this carefully.

Top Tips are useful hints and reminders that will help your child tackle different question types.

The Learning Papers cover key skills in shape connections, codes, completing a shape and spatial reasoning appropriate for children of this age. Bond Assessment Practice draw on a wide variety of skills and question types so that children are always challenged to think and do not get bored of answering same question type repeatedly. These books help children 'think on their feet' and cope with the unexpected.

Do not forget that a rounded education is key. As well as testing skills, the 11+ requires children to possess a wide vocabulary and robust general knowledge.

- Read a range of literature with your child – stories, poems, non-fiction, comics – it all counts.

- Experience new places together such as a visit to a museum or a walk through the woods.

New experiences can stimulate interesting discussions, deepen your child's understanding of the world, and help to build essential vocabulary.

- Play games together – card games, board games and sudokus are all excellent ways of developing key skills such as logical reasoning and problem solving and expanding your child's vocabulary.

NON-VERBAL REASONING SKILLS

This Bond 11+ Non-verbal Reasoning Assessment Practice book is useful for all 11+ exams. The learning papers cover the following key skills:

- **Shape connections** finding a common pattern of shapes, solving analogies, finding a shape most like another.
- **Completing a shape** solving matrices, adding or merging shapes.

The Mixed Papers ensure the key skills are consolidated thoroughly. Do not forget that a rounded education is key. Following a diagram to build a Lego model, drawing and colouring in mandala shapes, creating tessellations, making mosaic with tiles, making friendships bands or woven patterns, completing jigsaw puzzles, and playing with STEM toys are all fun ways of developing non-verbal reasoning skills. Hacker Can is a game that teaches computer programming and develops a logical way of thinking.

Each book is part of the Bond system with books increasing gradually in difficulty. If your child has an average score of 85% in this book, there is a clear progression in starting the next book level. If they have achieved an average score of 70% – 85%, then another book at this same level will provide further support. If your child has achieved an average score of less than 70%, then moving down a level will be most useful. Once your child has then developed the skills needed at this lower level, they can then move up with confidence. It is often better to begin at a lower level to build confidence as your child learns and develops their 11+ skills.

When tackling non-verbal reasoning questions it is good to think about shapes and their position, and angle of any part, also the number, shading and size of parts within the pattern. **SPANSS** can help you to remember this list:

Shape

Position

Angle

Number

Shading

Size

Learning Papers

1 Odd One Out

KEY SKILL

To find the odd one out, look carefully at all of the pictures or shapes. If there is a set of pictures, **identify** the objects first. Start by describing what they are **and** what they might be used for.

When the question has shapes or patterns, work through **SPANSS** to help find the odd one out.

WORKED EXAMPLES

Which is the odd one out? Circle the answer.

1

    a   b   c   d

Name each picture:

a is a cake
b is a sandwich
c is a spoon
d is a slice of pizza

Does anything link them all?
Yes, eating.
How are they linked with eating?

a a cake is food
b a sandwich is food
c a spoon is not food, it is used to eat food
d a slice of pizza is food

So **c** is the odd one out as it is not a type of food.

2

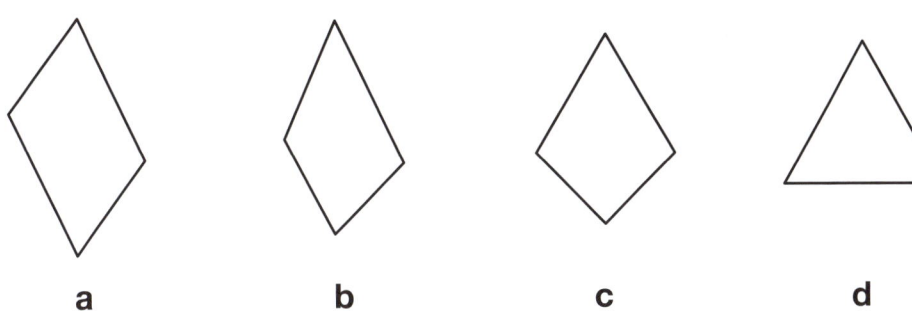

These are all simple shapes.

a is a shape with four sides
b is a shape with four sides
c is a shape with four sides
d is a triangle

So **d** is the odd one out because it is a different shape.

3

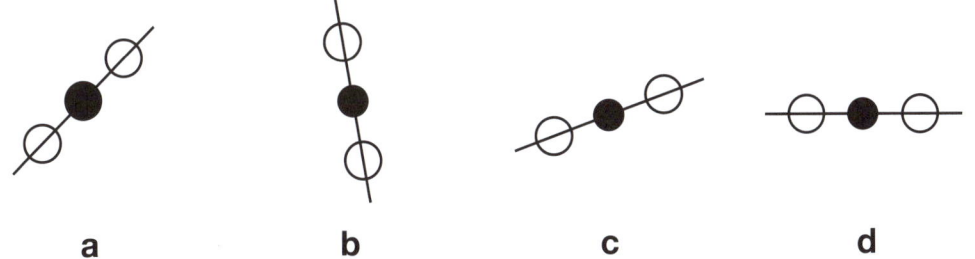

Here is a set of shapes making patterns. Using **SPANSS** can help to find the odd one out.

Shape	What shapes are used in each one? They all have circles, so that does not give an odd one out.
Position	In what position are the shapes in each pattern? They are all in a line, so that does not give an odd one out.
Angles	Are there different angles in the patterns? They are all at different angles, so that does not give an odd one out.
Number	How may circles in each pattern? They all have three circles, so that does not give an odd one out.
Shading	Are any parts shaded? They all have the middle circle shaded black, so that does not give an odd one out.

Size Are all parts the same size in each pattern?
a has three circles the same size, but **b**, **c** and **d** all have a small middle circle.

The odd one out is shape **a** because it is the only shape with a large circle in the middle.

Now try these.

Which is the odd one out? Circle the letter.

Then write down why that picture or shape is the odd one out.

1
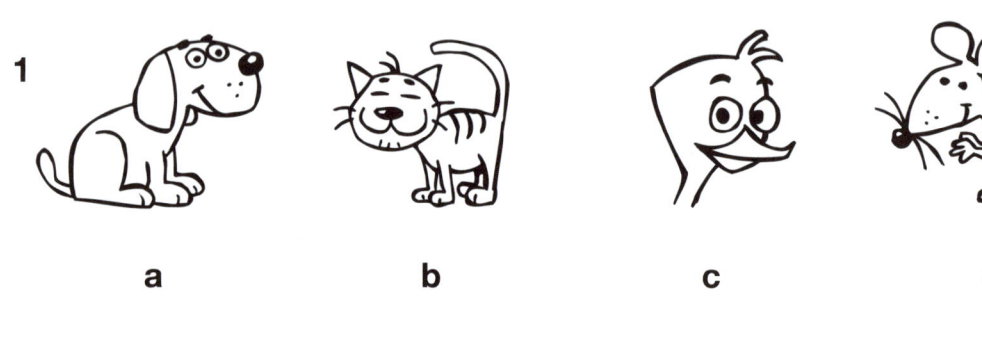
  a   b   c   d

Why? 1

2
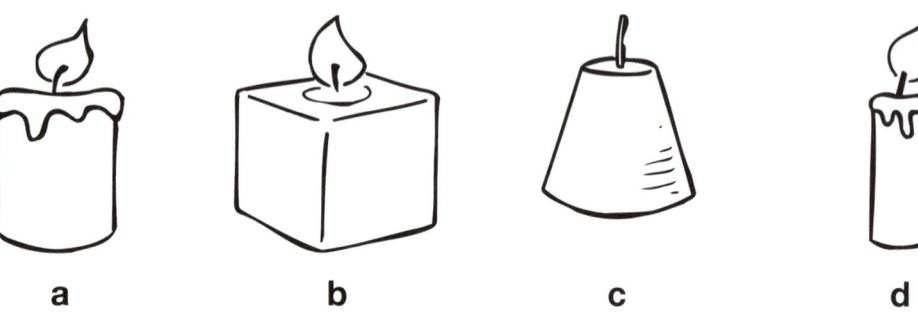
  a   b   c   d

Why? 1

3
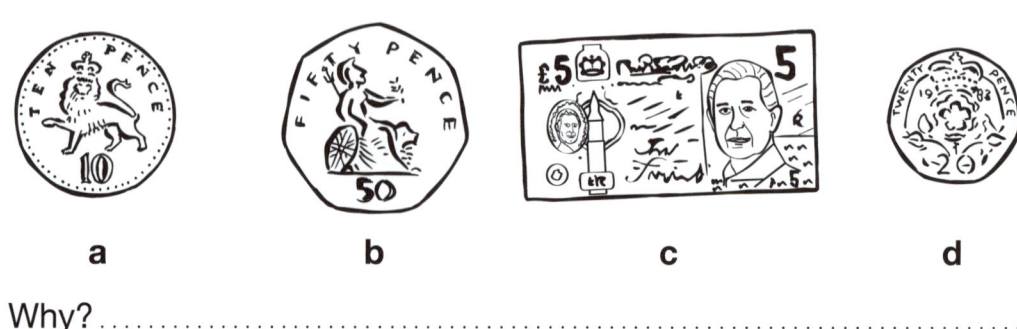
  a   b   c   d

Why? 1

4   a   b   c   d   e

Why? ....

5   a   b   c   d   e

Why? ....

6   a   b   c   d

Why? ....

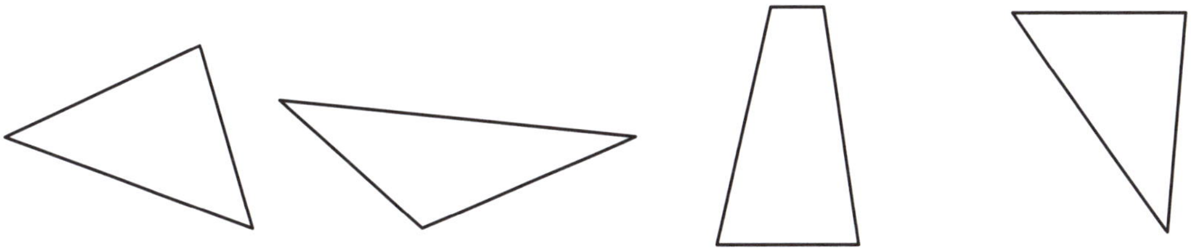

7   a   b   c   d

Why? ....

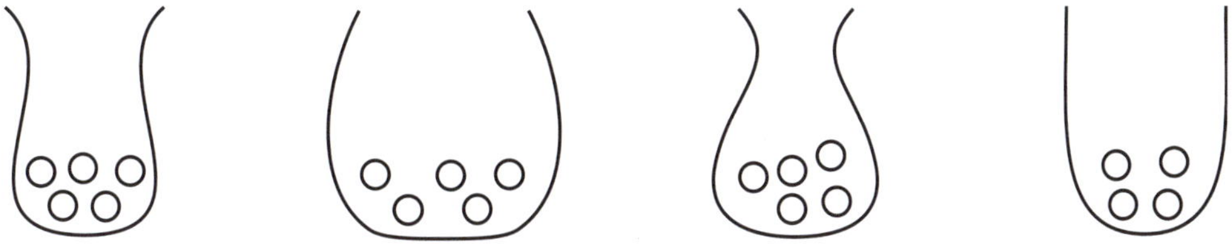

Odd One Out

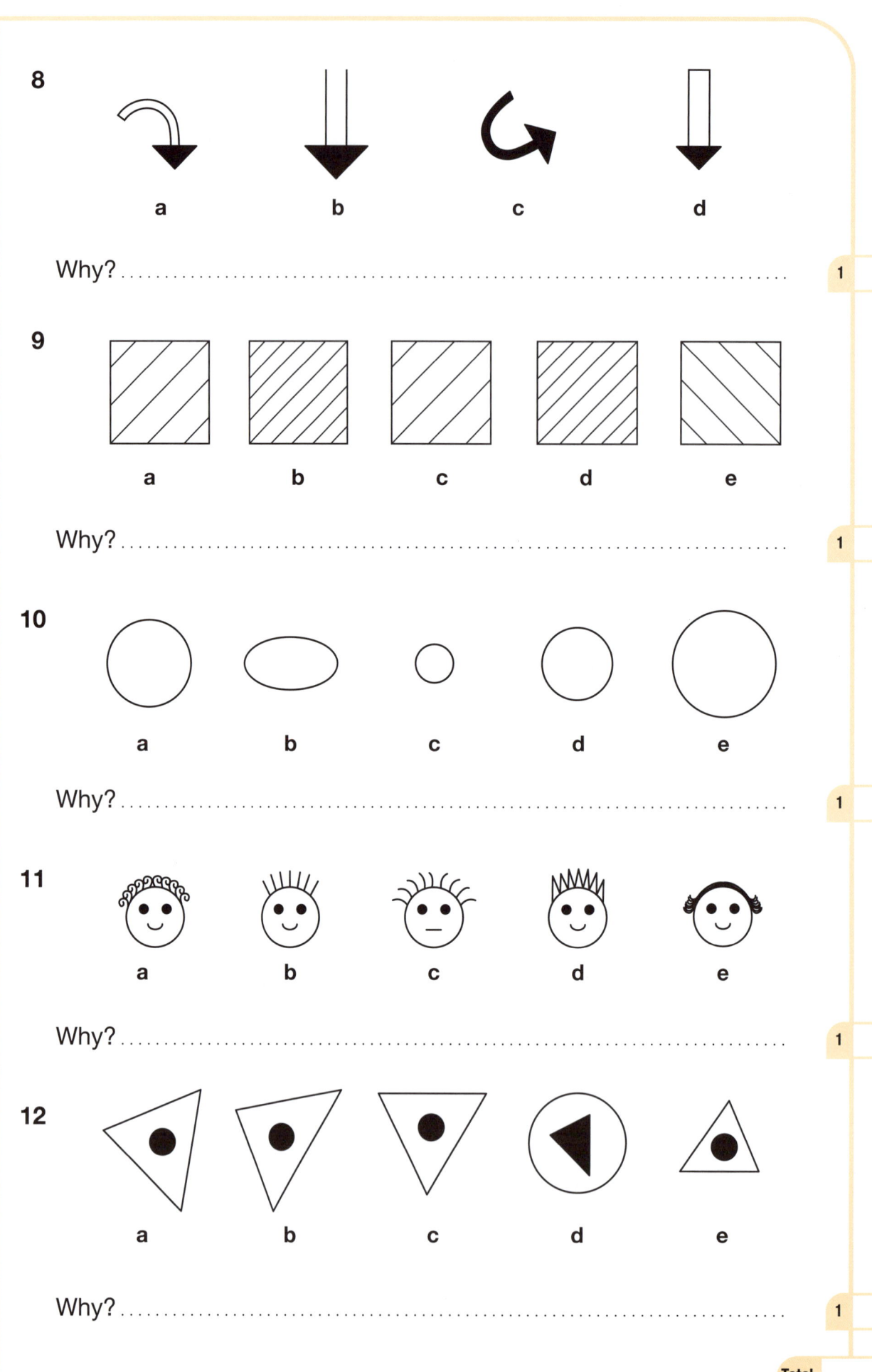

2 Series

KEY SKILL

In these questions, the goal is to look at a line of pictures or shapes and work out which picture or shape comes next.

The pictures or shapes may be:

- arranged to give a repeating pattern
- showing a story or process
- increasing or decreasing along the line.

WORKED EXAMPLES

Which one comes next?

- Find where the first picture or shape is repeated along the line, then number all of the sequence from the beginning up to that point.
- When the repeating pattern is found, work out which picture or shape is next.

In this example look carefully along the row of shapes:
heart–circle–square–heart–circle …
It is a repeating pattern made up of three shapes –heart–circle–square–.
Now assign a number to the shapes that are repeated:

TOP TIP!

There can be any number of shapes in a repeating sequence so look carefully along the line.

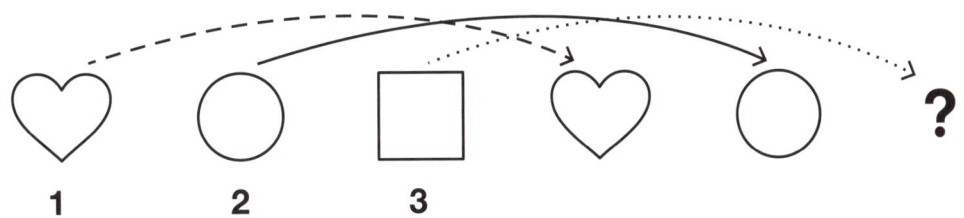

The heart and the circle are repeated, so the next shape in the sequence is the square, so **option c** is the answer.

> **TOP TIP!**
> The number of shapes in the repeated part can vary – watch out for repeated shapes within the sequence!

2

- If the pictures are telling a story or showing a process, describe what they show.

- Look at the answer options carefully – more than one of them might be showing something that happens after the last picture, so think logically to decide which would come next.

Describe the story so far:
- A girl has a balloon in her hand.
- She starts to blow it up.
- The balloon gets bigger as she blows.

Now look at the answer options and describe what they show:
a balloon getting bigger still
b balloon before it is blown up
c girl with three balloons
d girl walking away with three balloons

Could any of these come next? Options a, c and d could all come next but not b, so cross it out.

Then think about the sequence – she has to finish blowing up one balloon before having three in her hand.

Option **a** has one balloon, which is bigger than the last picture given, so **option a** is the answer.

3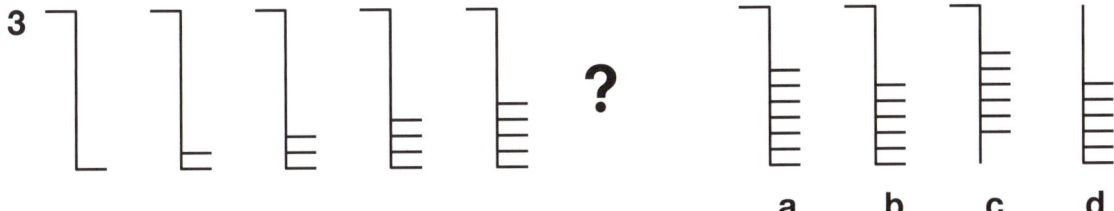

- Part or all of a shape may be increasing or decreasing along the line.
- The change may be in the length, number or angle.
- Use SPANSS to see what is changing and how this can help to find the next shape in the sequence.

Describe the first pattern:
A **vertical** line, with a short line to the left at the top and one short line to the right at the bottom.

And the next pattern:
A vertical line, with a short line to the left at the top and two short lines to the right at the bottom.

What has changed? The number of lines to the right at the bottom.

- Does the number continue to increase along the sequence? Yes, one more is added each time.
- Carefully count the number of lines in the last shape: five

So the next pattern will have six lines to the right at the bottom and one line to the left at the top.

Check the answer options:

> **TOP TIP!**
>
> Remember to cross out an option as soon as it is clear that it is not right.

a has seven lines to the right, not six, so cross it out
b has six lines to the right, looks right – check the other options
c does not have a line at the very bottom, so cross it out
d does not have a line at the top, so cross it out

So **option b** is the answer.

> **TOP TIP!**
>
> Variations! This sort of question can get trickier when more than one of these elements is included, such as combining a set of alternating shapes with an increasing number, or a picture story where one part is decreasing in number. Just look carefully and describe accurately what is in the series given and then work out the next pattern.

Now try these.

Which one comes next? Circle the letter.

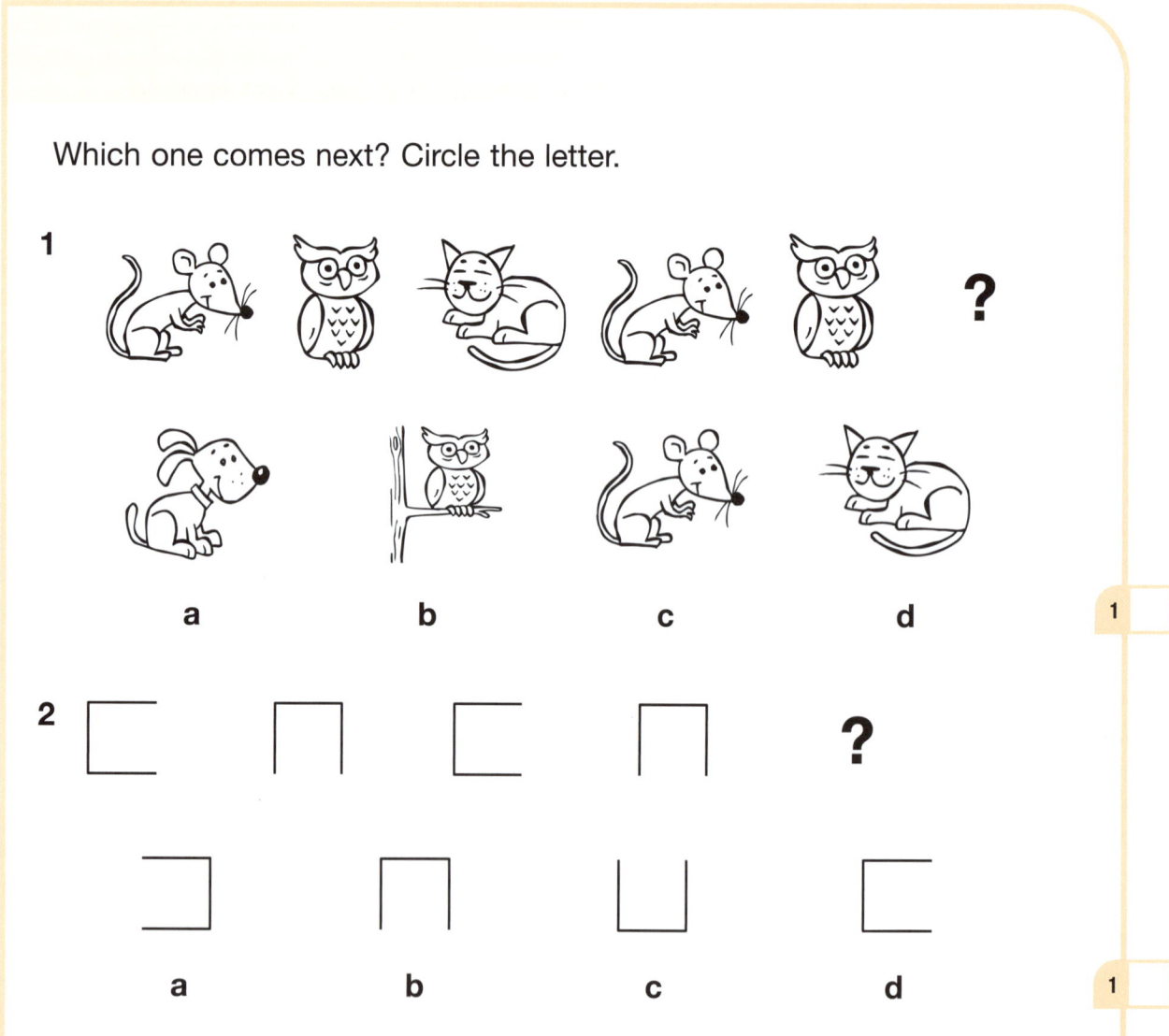

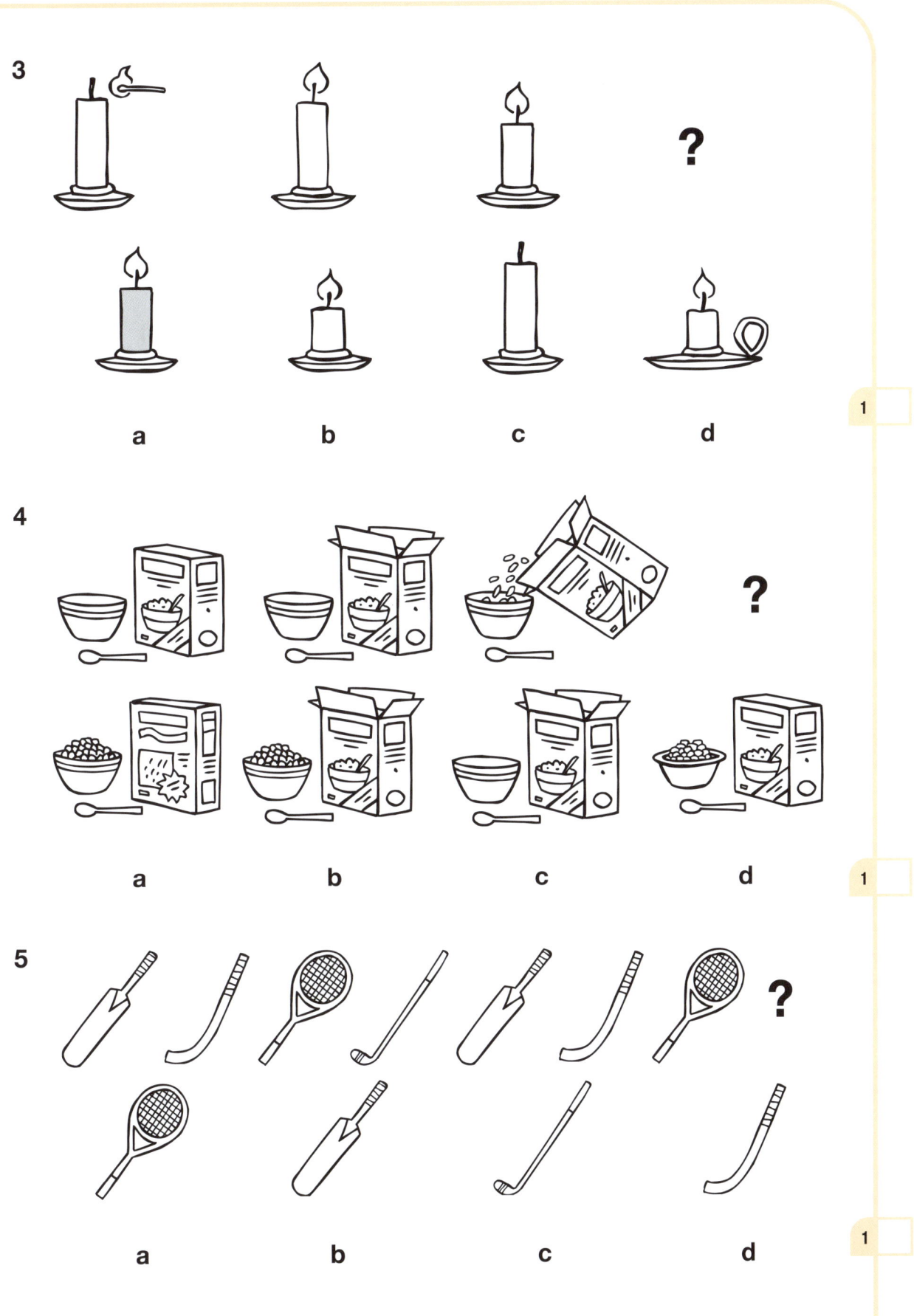

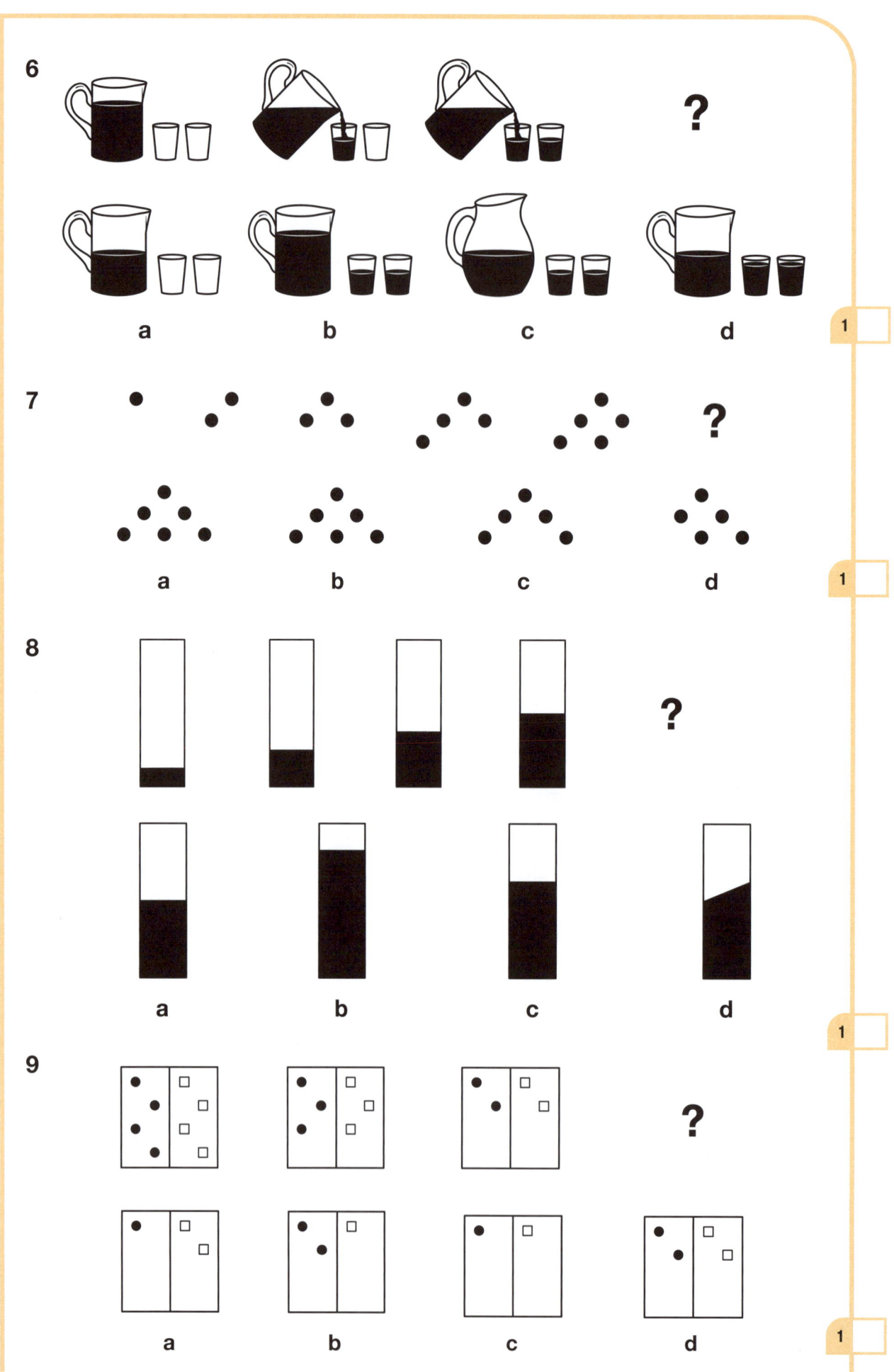

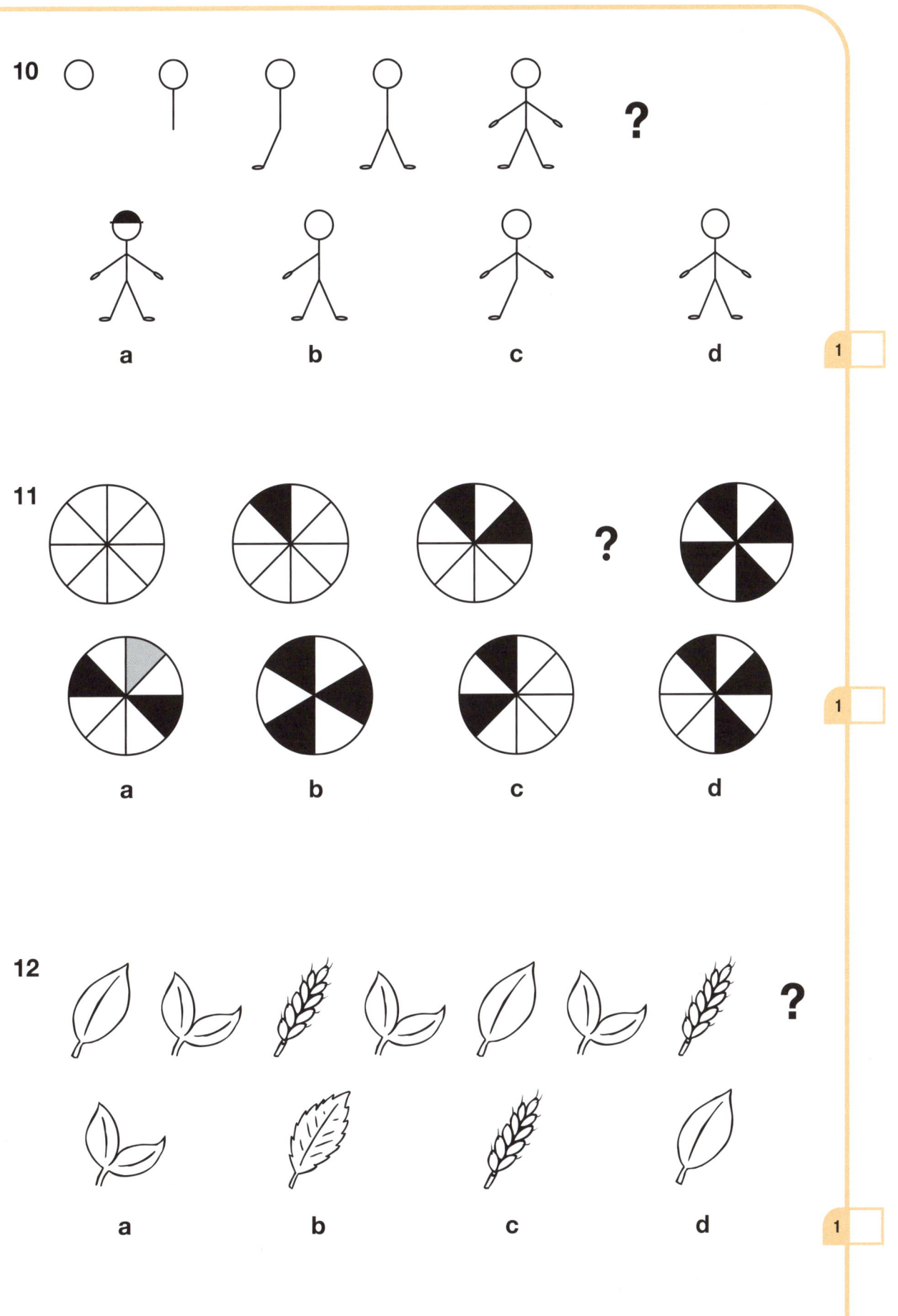

3 Similarities

> **KEY SKILL**
>
> Which one belongs?
>
> To answer these questions, look at the group of shapes or patterns on the left and work out how they are similar. Then look at the answer options to find the one that is similar to the shapes or patterns in the group. Using SPANSS can help identify how the different shapes in a group are similar to each other. If the group has objects rather than shapes, look carefully and describe each one to find out how they are similar.

WORKED EXAMPLES

1 Which one belongs to the group on the left?

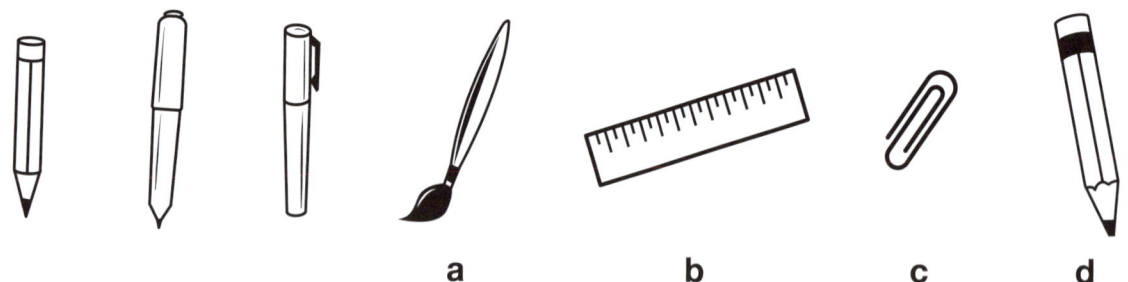

In this question the group on the left is made up of objects, so describe them to see how they are similar:
- a pencil – used for writing and drawing
- a biro – used for mostly writing
- a pen – used for writing.

All of the objects are used for writing. Now look at the answer options:
a a paintbrush, used for painting
b a ruler, used for lines or measuring
c a paperclip, used for clipping paper together
d a pencil, used for writing

So **option d** is the answer.

2

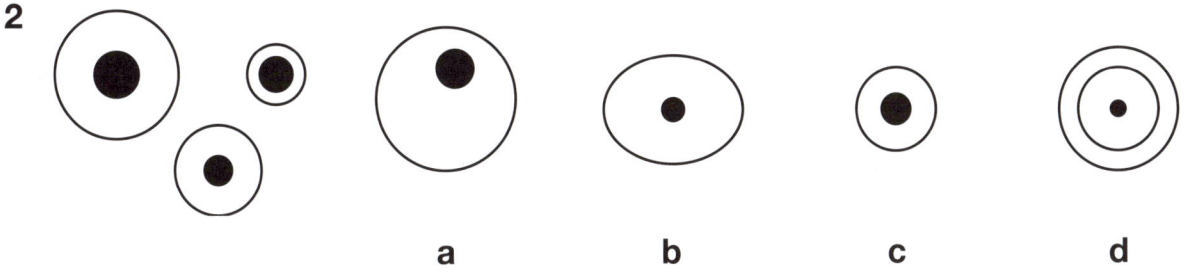

                      a   b   c   d

Look at the shapes on the left and work through SPANSS to find how they are similar:

Shape   They are all circles.
Position   They have smaller circles in the middle of the larger circles.
Angle   There are no angles.
Number   They all have two circles.
Shading   The middle circle is black.
Size   The sizes are all different.

Now look at the answer options to see which one best matches the group.

TOP TIP!

Remember to cross out an answer option as soon as you find it cannot be correct.

---

a The black circle is not in the middle of the larger circle, so it can be crossed out.
b The outer shape is an oval, not a circle, so it can be crossed out.
c This option has two circles with a black one in the middle of the larger one, so it is possible that this is the answer. Check the final option.
d There are three circles so this can be crossed out.

So **option c** is the answer.

Similarities

3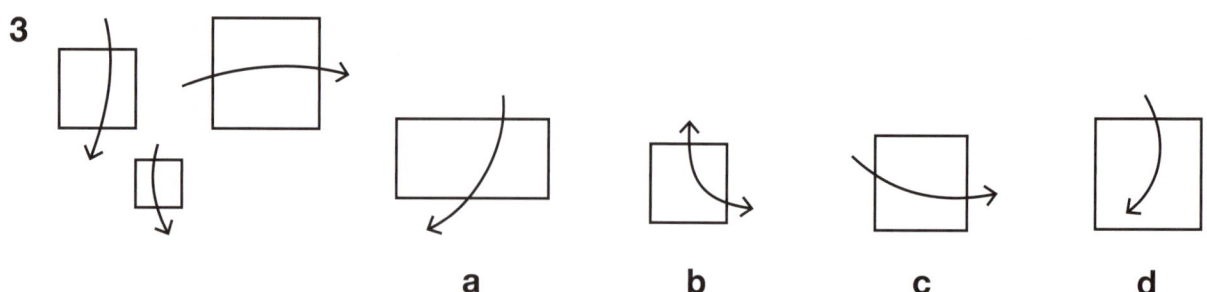

Look at the shapes on the left and work through SPANSS to find how they are similar:

Shape   They are all squares.
Position   The arrow crosses the square.
Angle   The arrow is curved with no sharp angles.
Number   There is an arrowhead at one end.
Shading   There is no shading.
Size   The sizes are all different.

Now look at the answer options to see which one best matches the group.

a This option is a rectangle not a square, so cross it out.
b The arrow has two arrowheads, not one, so cross it out.
c This option is a square crossed by a curved arrow with one arrowhead, so it is possible that this is the answer. Check the final option.
d The curved arrow does not fully cross the square, so cross it out.

So **option c** is the answer.

Now try these.

Which one belongs to the group on the left? Circle the answer.

1.   a   b   c   d

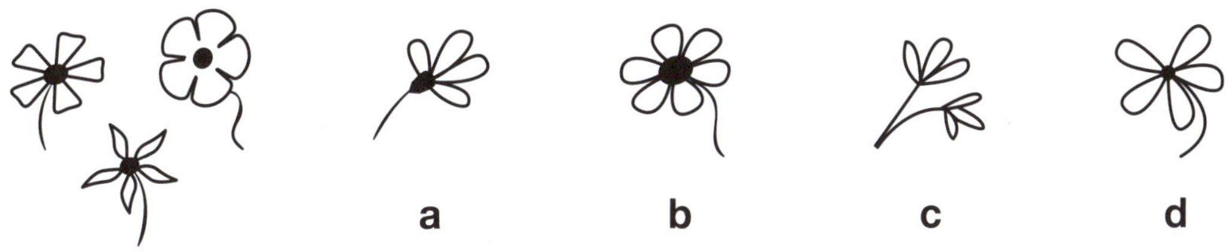

2.   a   b   c   d

3.   a   b   c   d

4.   a   b   c   d

5.   a   b   c   d

6.   a   b   c   d

Similarities

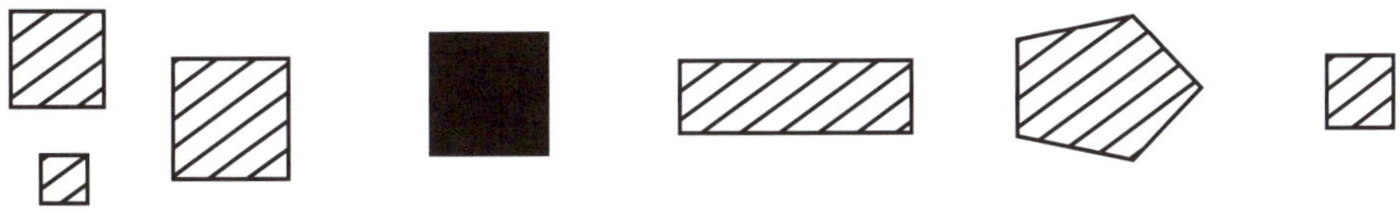

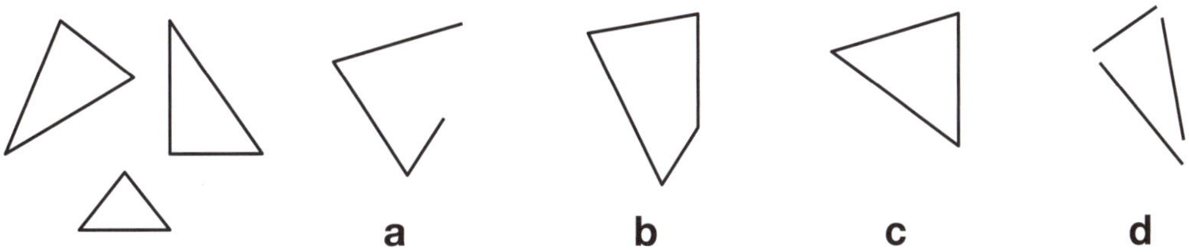

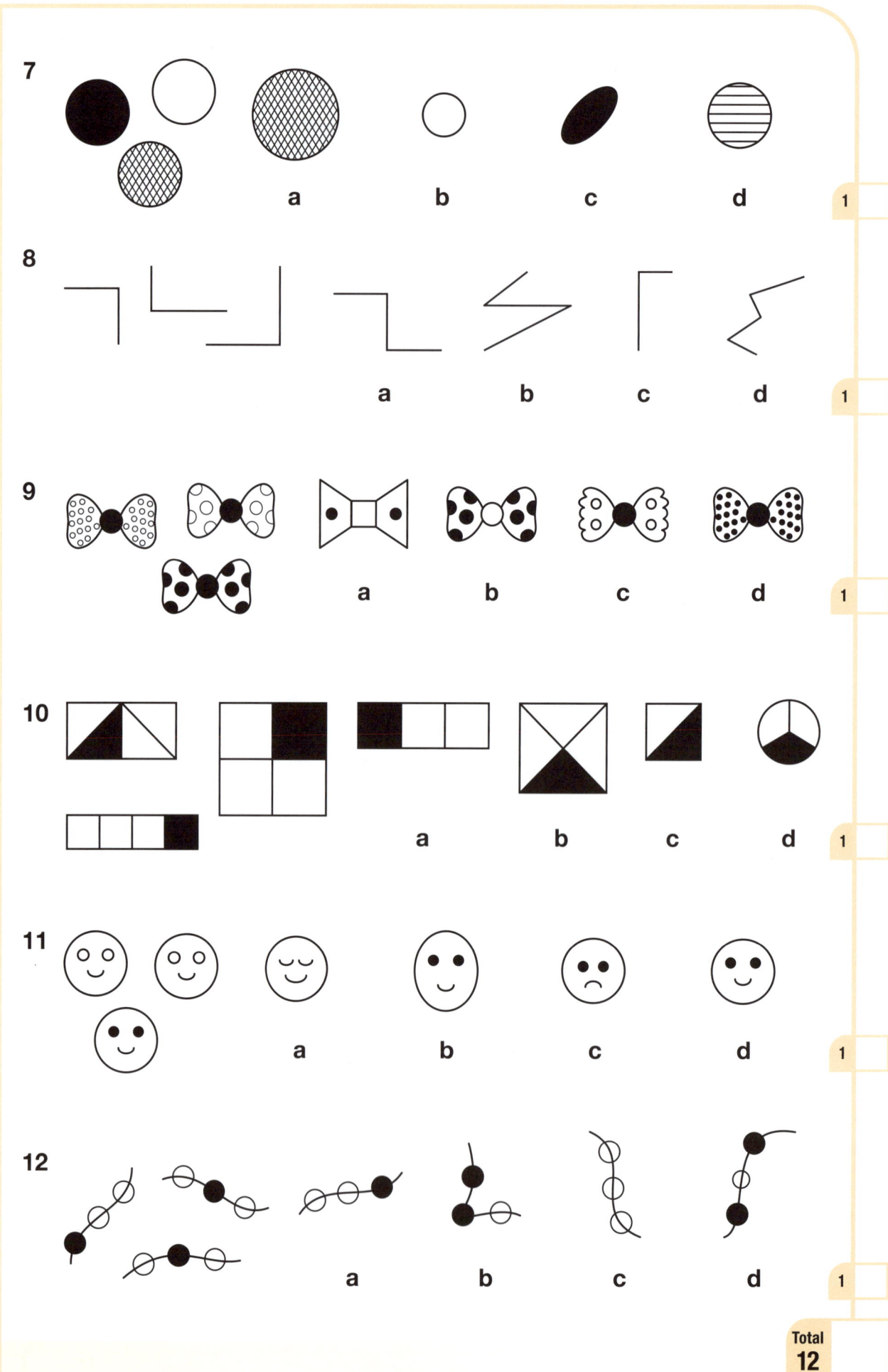

4 Missing Pieces

KEY SKILL

In these questions there is a pattern set out in a grid and the goal is to find the missing piece. The grid may be made up of four squares or nine squares. There may be a repeating pattern along the rows or down the columns. By looking at the rows or columns that are complete, the pattern can be worked out. Then draw the missing shape in the space and match this to the answer options given. The whole grid might be one big pattern, where one half is a **reflection** of the other half. Again, it is helpful to draw what the missing part should look like in the space to complete the pattern. This can then be matched to the answer options.

WORKED EXAMPLES

Which one completes the pattern?

1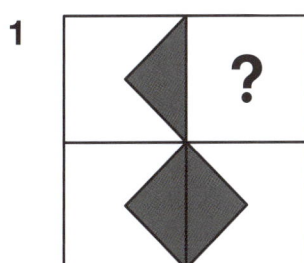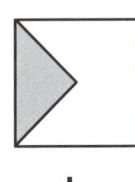
          a   b   c   d

Looking at the left side of this grid, it is clear that the shape is the same in both the top and the bottom squares.
To complete the grid, copy the shape that is in the bottom right square into the top right square.
This gives a whole pattern of two shaded diamonds.

Now look at the answer options:
a The triangle is on the wrong side, so cross it out.
b The shading is wrong, so cross it out.
c The triangle is in the same position as the square below, so it is a possible answer. Check the final option.
d The triangle is along the base of the square rather than at the side, so cross it out.

So **option c** is the answer.

2

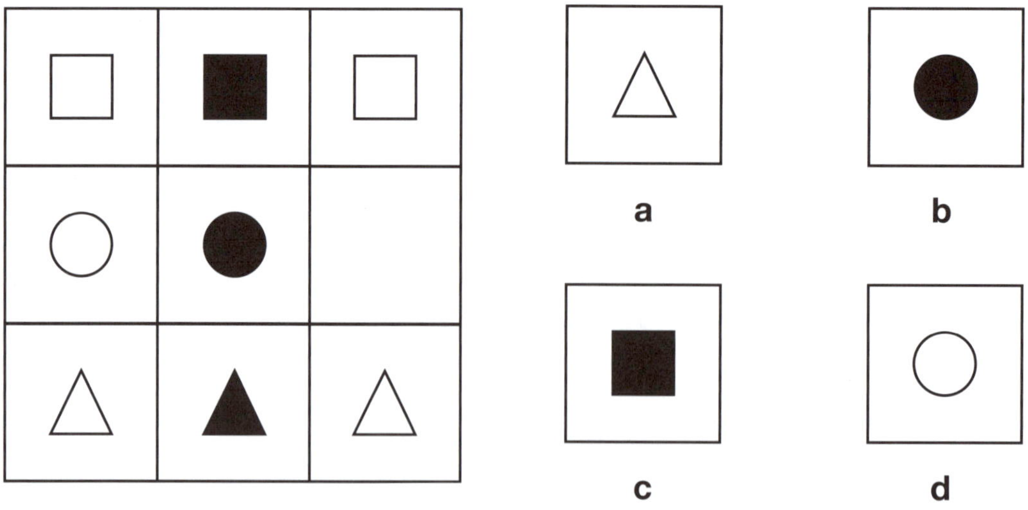

The top and bottom row are complete so look along them to find the pattern. SPANSS can help.

Along each row, what do you notice about:

Shape The shape is always the same along a row.
Position The shape is always in the middle of the square.
Angle There are no variations in angle.
Number There is one shape in each square.
Shading The pattern goes white–black–white.
Size The shapes are all the same size.

Cross out options a and c which are not circles!

There will be one circle in the middle of the square, so b and d are possible answers.
The first two circles go white–black– so the next shape will be white. Option b, which has a black circle, can now be crossed out.

This gives **option d**, the white circle, as the correct answer.

Notice that looking at the columns would have given the same answer:
- Each column goes square, circle, triangle from top to bottom.
- All the shapes in one column are the same colour.
- Each square in the columns has one shape in the middle of the square.

TOP TIP!

If a grid pattern looks tricky, checking along the rows and down the columns will help to find the pattern.

3

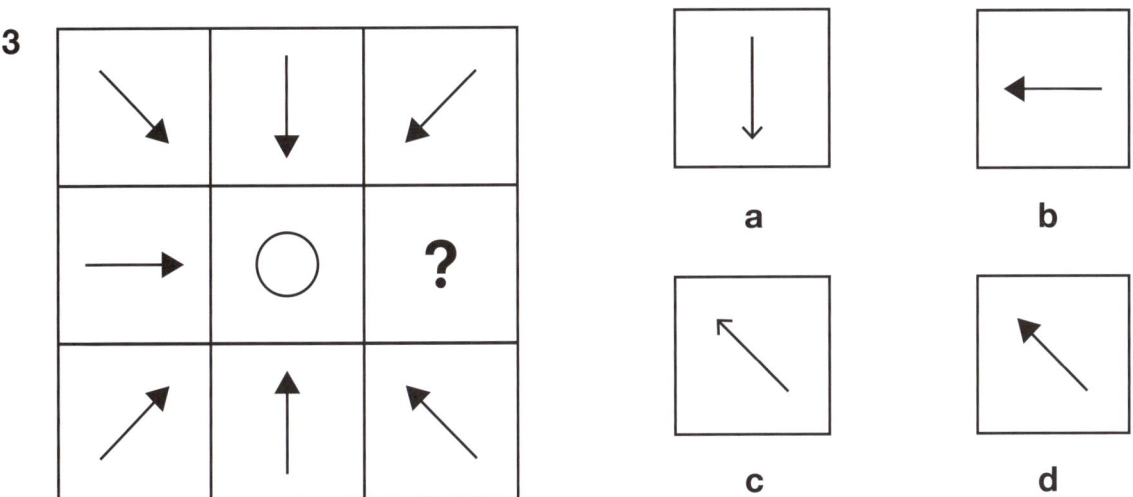

This is an example where the whole grid forms a pattern, so start by describing the pattern.
- There are arrows in the squares around the edge of the grid.
- The arrows are all the same style.
- The arrows all point to the centre.

From this description, work out that the missing square will have:
- an arrow pointing to the centre, **horizontal** and pointing left
- a white arrowhead.

Draw in the missing arrow and compare to the answer options:
a The arrow is not horizontal, so cross it out.
b The arrow is horizontal, pointing left and has a black arrowhead, looks possible. Check other options.
c The arrow is not horizontal, so cross it out.
d The arrow is not horizontal, so cross it out.

So **option b** is the correct answer.

Now try these and write down why each one completes the pattern.

Which one completes the pattern? Circle the answer.

1 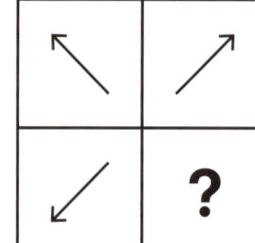   a   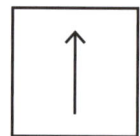   b   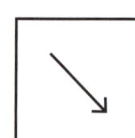   c   d

Why? ....

2 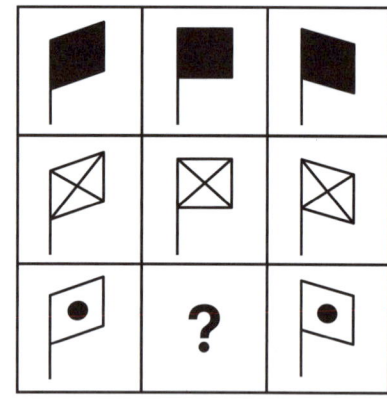   a   b

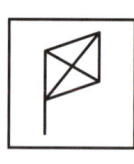   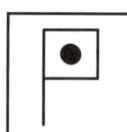

c   d

Why? ....

3 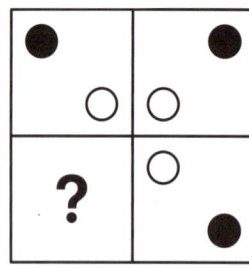   a 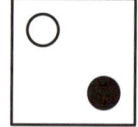   b   c 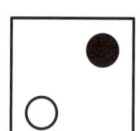   d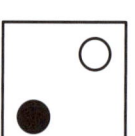

Why? ....

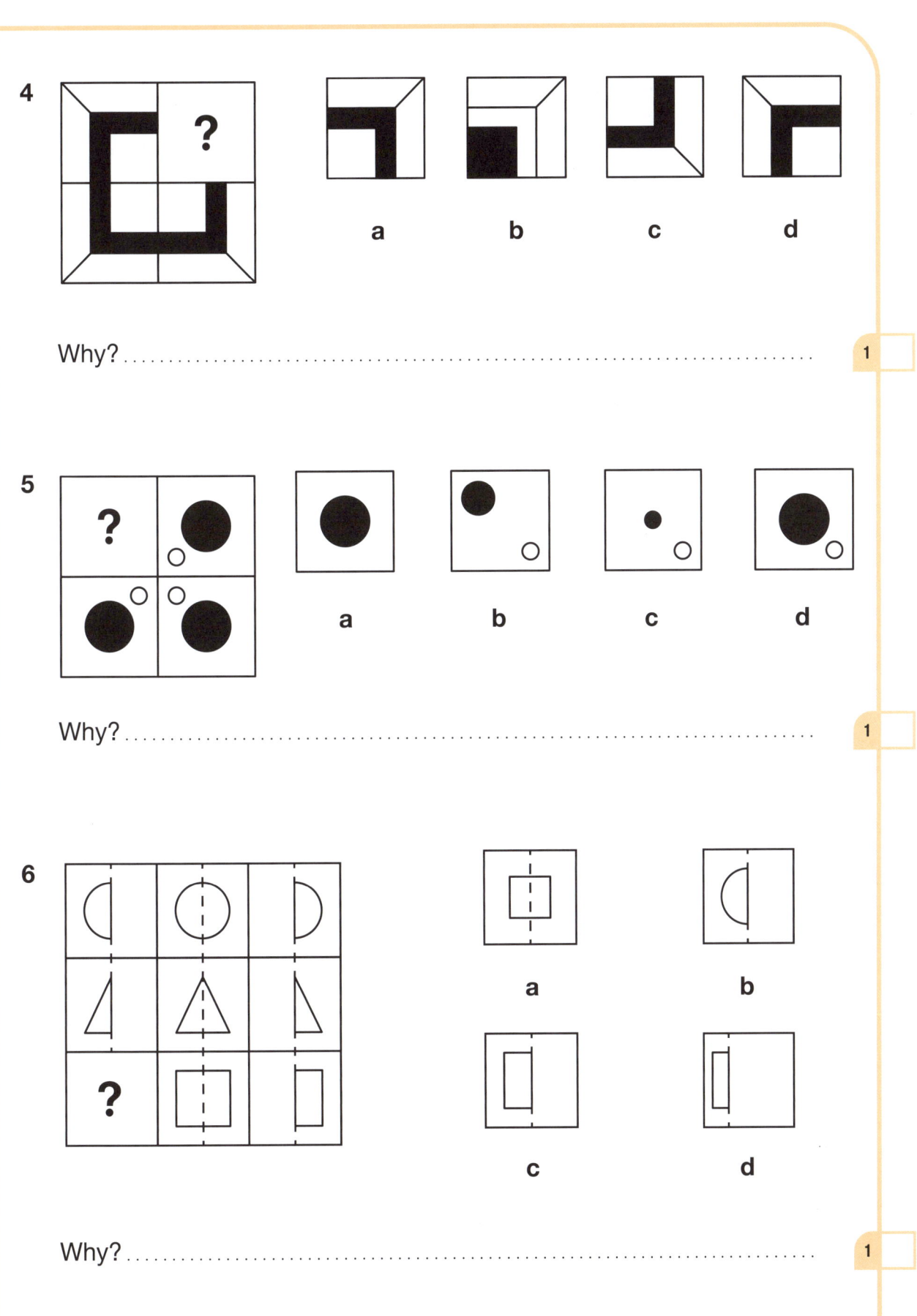

7

Why? ....

8

Why? ....

9

Why? ....

30

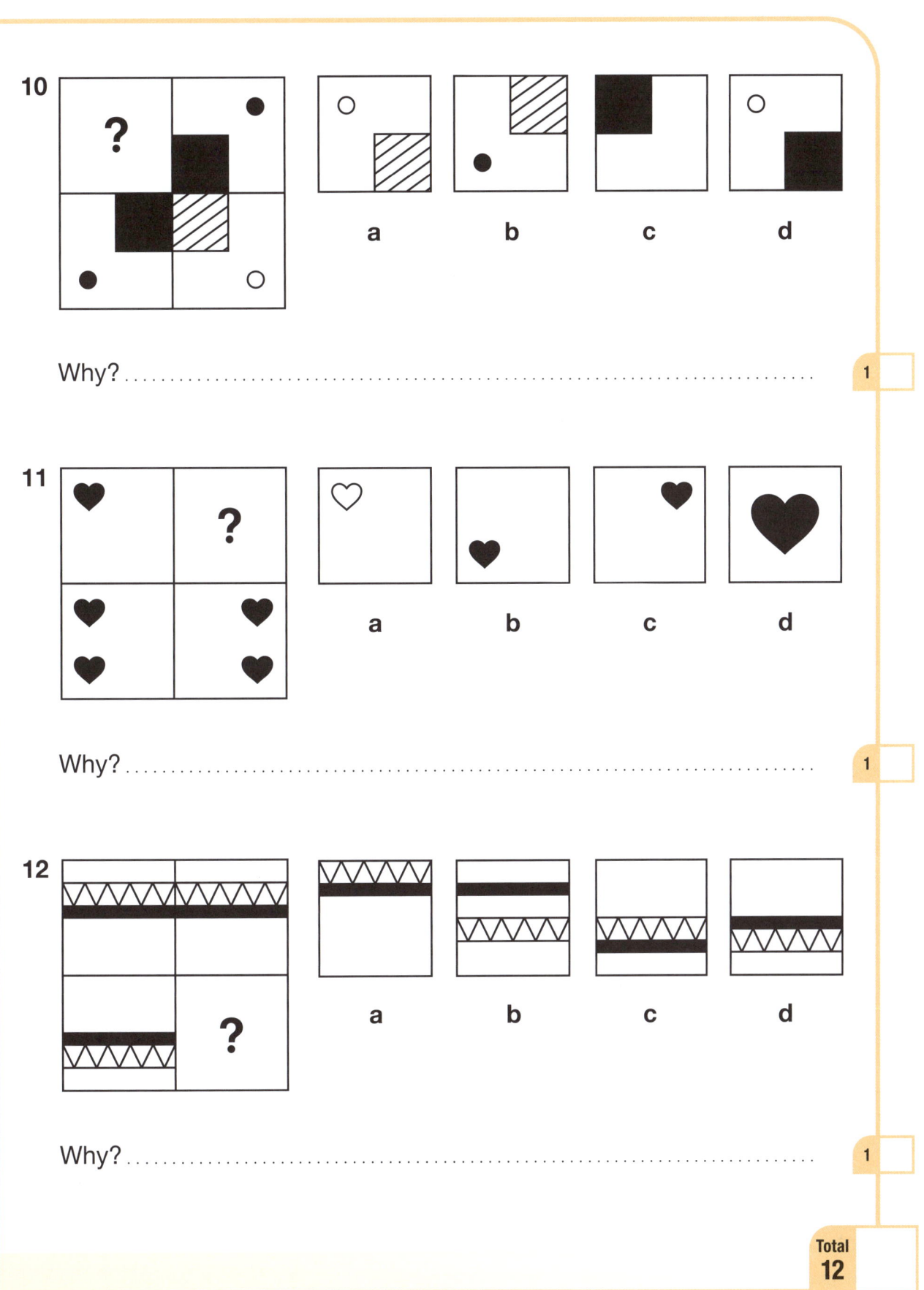

5 Analogies

KEY SKILL

In these questions the goal is to work out the connection between the first pair of pictures or shapes. Then complete the second pair of pictures or shapes using the same connection.

- With picture questions, start by describing the first two pictures and working out the link between them.
- Using SPANSS is a good way to work out the connections between shapes and patterns.

> **TOP TIP!**
>
> Remember SPANSS stands for Shape, Position, Angle, Number, Shading, Size!

WORKED EXAMPLES

Which one completes the second pair in the same way as the first pair?

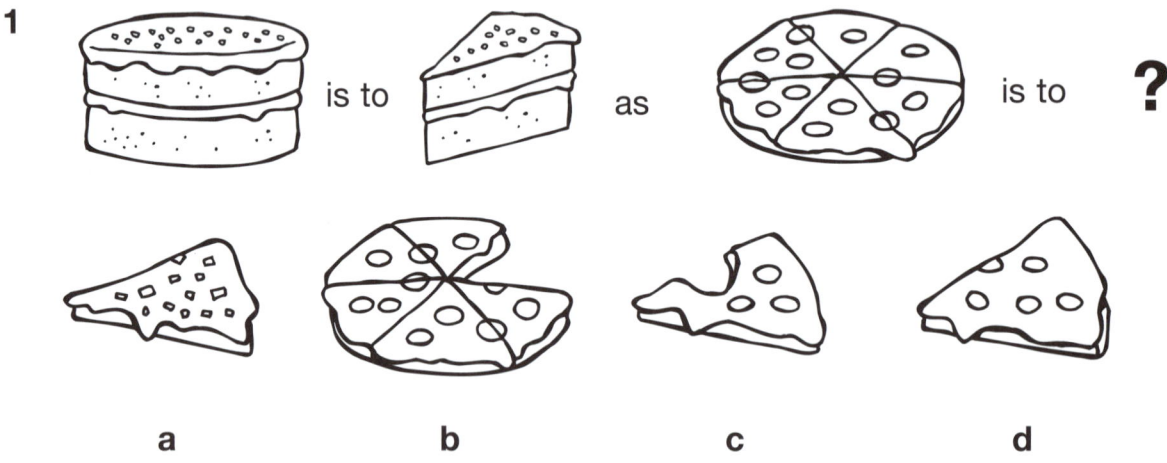

1

a   b   c   d

This question has a set of pictures so start by describing the first pair of pictures.

There is a whole large cake and then a picture of a slice of cake, which is part of the whole.

The next picture is a whole pizza.

Using the same connection as between the two cake pictures, the second pair of pictures will be completed by a slice of pizza that is part of the whole.

Now look at the answer options in turn:

a Option **a** is a slice of pizza, a possible answer. Check the rest of the options.
b Option **b** is made up of five slices of pizza, so this is not correct and can be crossed out.
c Option **c** is a slice of pizza with a bite taken out of it, but in the first pair of pictures there was no bite taken out of the slice of cake. This is not the answer, so cross it out.
d Option **d** is a slice of pizza, a possible answer.

As both option **a** and option **d** appear to be possible answers, look at the detail of the pictures. How are they different from each other?
The pizza toppings are different shapes and sizes – they are small and square in option **a** and larger circles in option **d**.
Looking at the picture of the whole pizza, which type of topping does the original picture have?
It has larger circles, so **option d** is the correct answer.

2

Here is another set of pictures. Describe the first pair and look for the connection between them.
A picture of rain and a pair of wellington boots – the connection is that the boots are footwear you might use in the rain.

Now look at the first picture of the second pair – it shows sunshine. Using the same connection, what might you wear when it is hot and sunny?

Now look at the answer options in turn:

a Option **a** is an ice cream – lovely in hot weather but cannot be worn, so cross it out.

b Option **b** is a cold drink – also good on a hot day, but cannot be worn, so cross it out.

c Option **c** is a warm coat – can be worn, but not on a hot day, so cross it out.

d Option **d** is a pair of sandals – good on a hot day and can be worn.

So **option d** is the correct answer.

TOP TIP!

Do not allow other connections between pictures to distract you! Notice how options a and b do go well with a hot sunny day and could be chosen by mistake! Always remember that the connection must be the same as the connection shown between the first pair of pictures.

3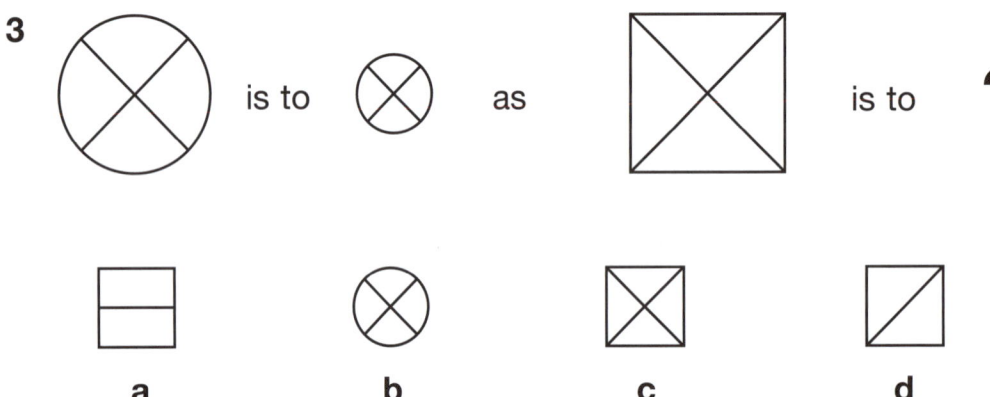

This question has shapes rather than pictures. Look at the first pair of shapes then use SPANSS to find the connection between them.

Shape	They are both circles, so the shape does not change.
Position	The crosses are inside the circles.
Angle	The lines form a diagonal cross, an X pattern, in both shapes.
Number	There is no change in the number of lines.
Shading	There is no shading.
Size	The first shape is large and the second shape is small.

Using the same connections, what will complete the second pair?
- The first shape is a square and the shape does not change, so the answer will be a square. You can now cross out option **b**.
- The first shape has an X inside, so the second shape will also have an X inside. You can now cross out options **a** and **d**.
- That leaves option **c** for the correct answer – check it. The first shape is a large square, so the second shape will be a small square.

Option **c** is a small square, so **c** is the correct answer.

Now try these.

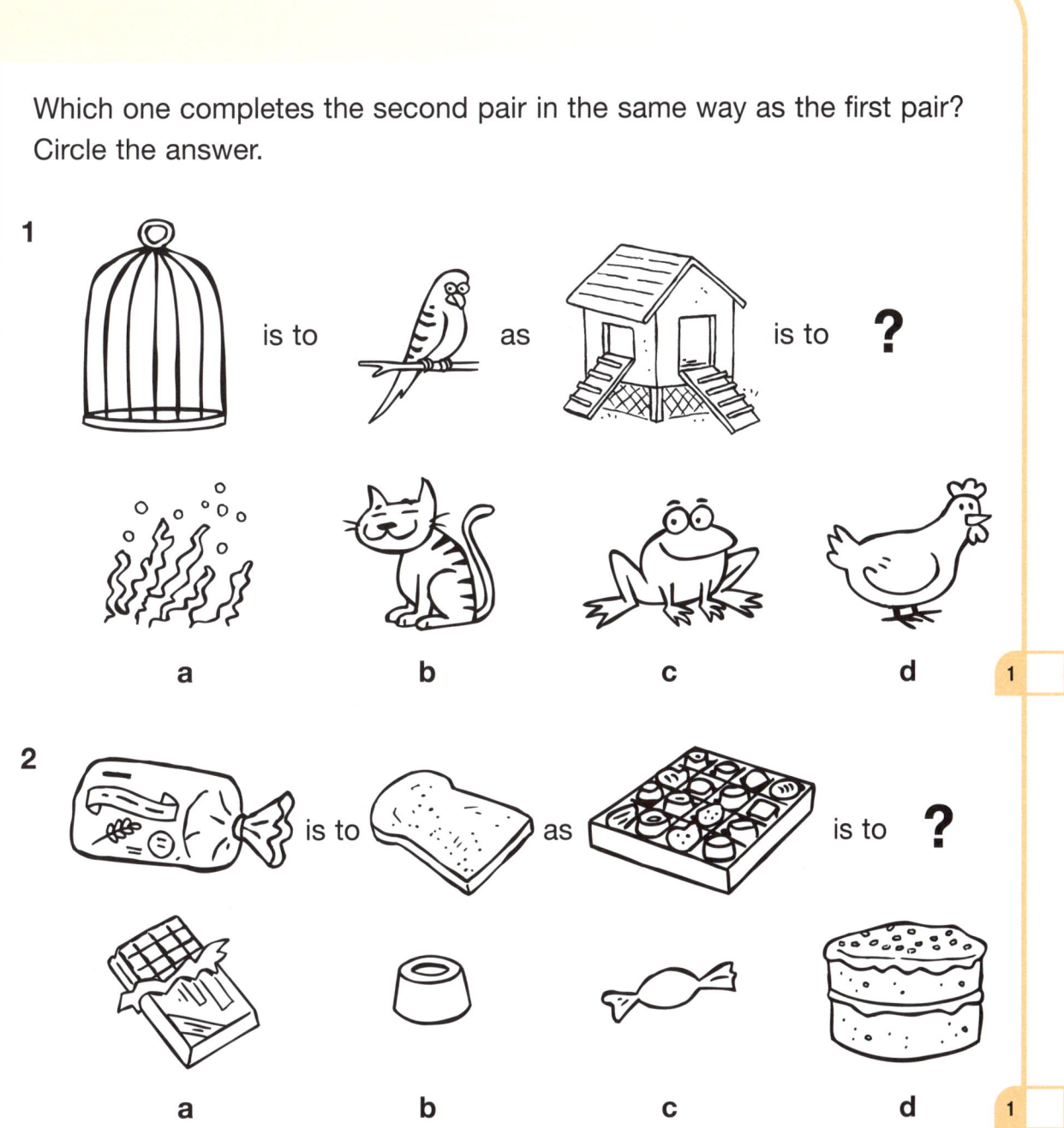

Which one completes the second pair in the same way as the first pair? Circle the answer.

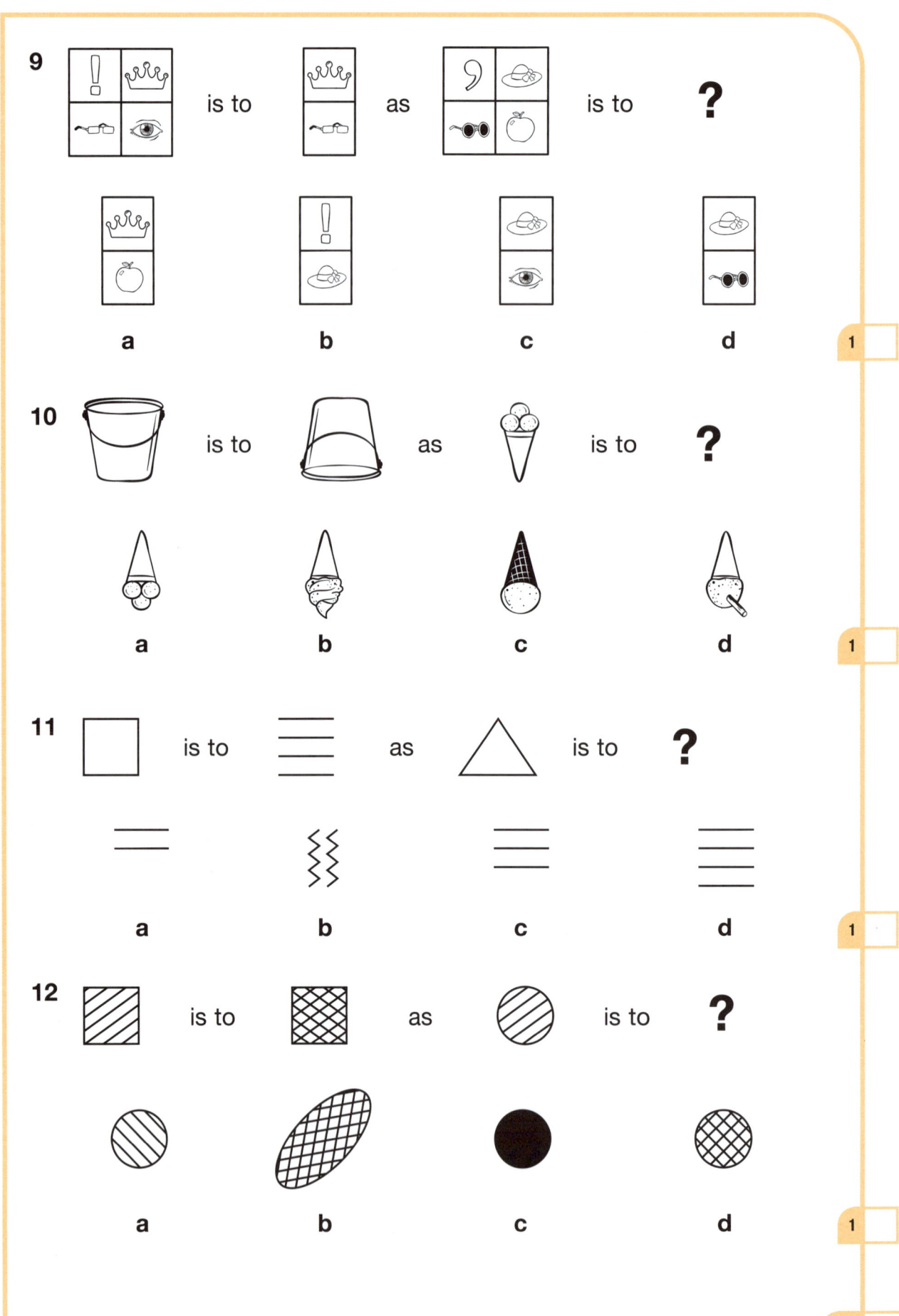

6 Hidden Shape

> **KEY SKILL**
>
> In these questions, a small shape is hidden inside one of the larger patterns or shapes. The goal is to find which one it is hidden in. Start by describing the smaller shape that is hidden. Then look very carefully at the detail in each answer option. The shape will not change size.
>
> The shape may be an object – but still look at it carefully and describe it. When the shape is an object, some of the answer options given can be distracting as they are linked in some way to the object, but do not have the object hidden within them, so take care and look closely at the detail of each option!

WORKED EXAMPLES

In which shape on the right is the shape on the left hidden?

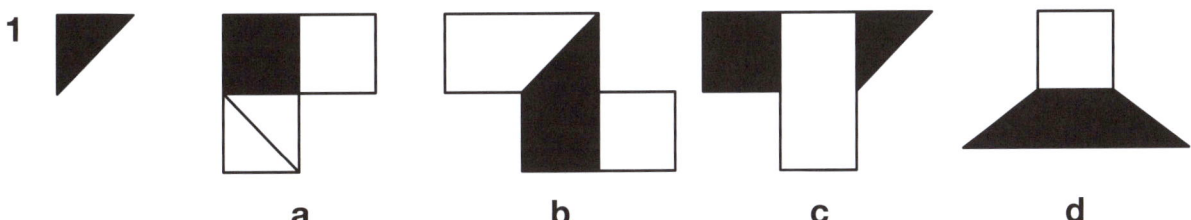

First describe the shape:
The small shape hiding within a larger one is a shaded triangle with a square corner at the top left.

The hidden shape is shaded so check the shaded shapes in each answer option.

Is the shaded part a triangle with a square corner at the top left?
a No, the shaded part is a square.
b No, the shaded part is a four-sided shape not a triangle.
c Yes, one of the shaded parts is a triangle with a square corner at the top left – a possible answer. Check the other options.
d No, the shaded part is a four-sided shape not a triangle.

So **option c** is the answer.

2 In which shape on the right is the shape on the left hidden?

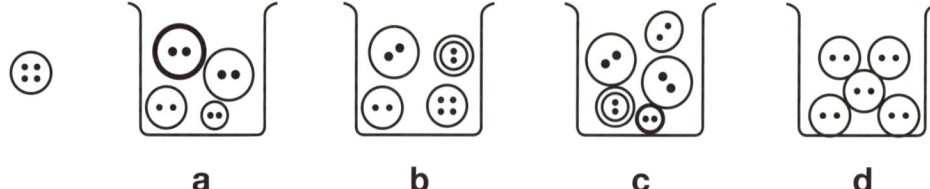

The shape hiding in the larger shapes is a small circle with four spots inside it.

All of the answer options have small circles within them.
The circles all have spots within them.

Now look carefully at each one to find the one which is a small circle that has four spots inside it.
a No, all of the circles in this one have two spots, so cross it out.
b Yes, the small circle at the bottom right has four spots – a possible answer. Check the other options.
c No, all of the circles in this one have two spots, so cross it out.
d No, all of the circles in this one have two spots, so cross it out.

So **option b** is the answer.

Now try these.

In which shape on the right is the shape on the left hidden?
Circle the answer.

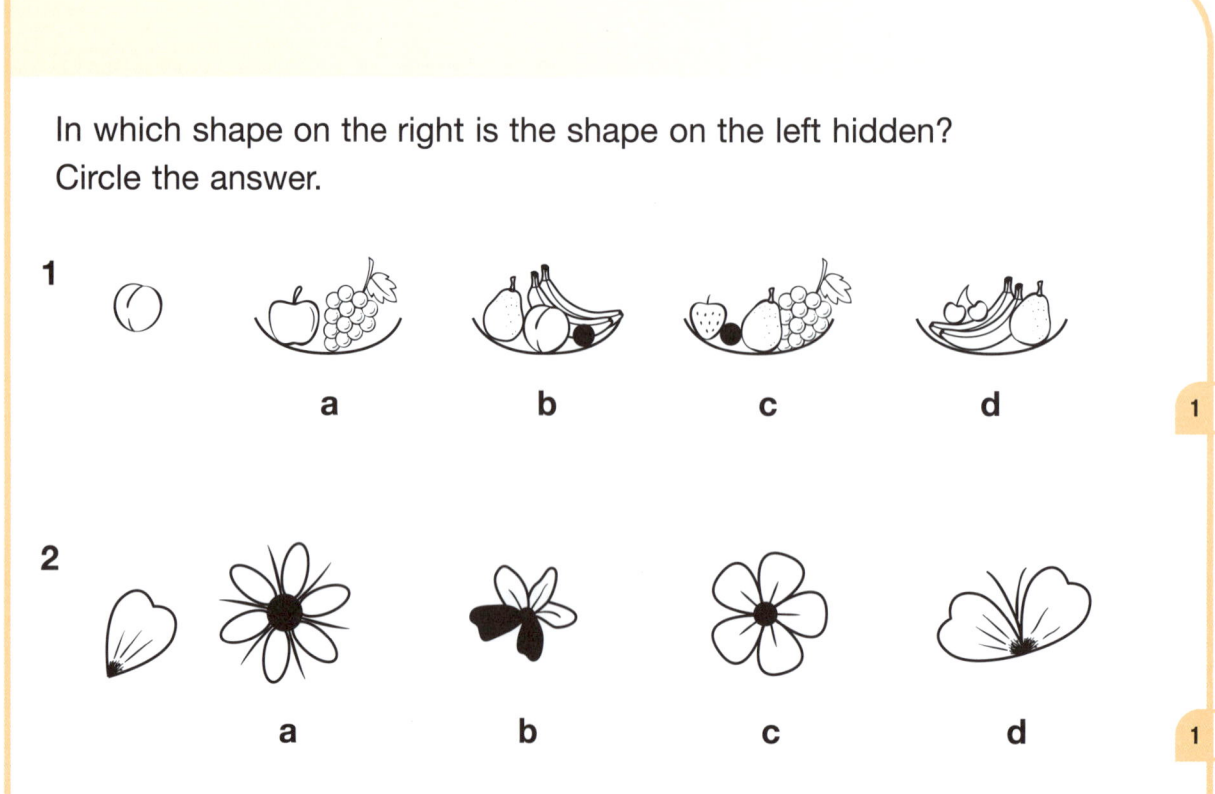

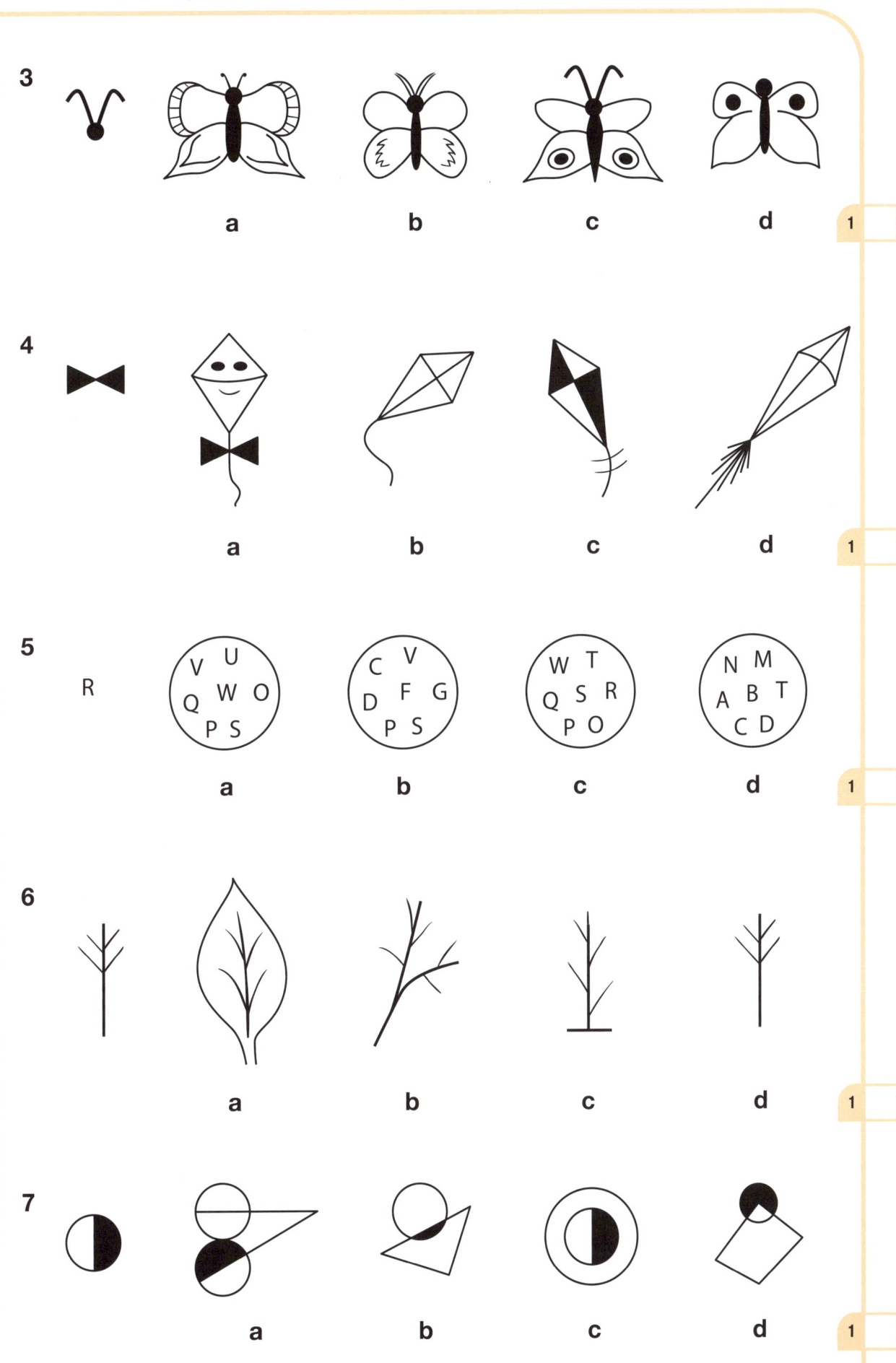

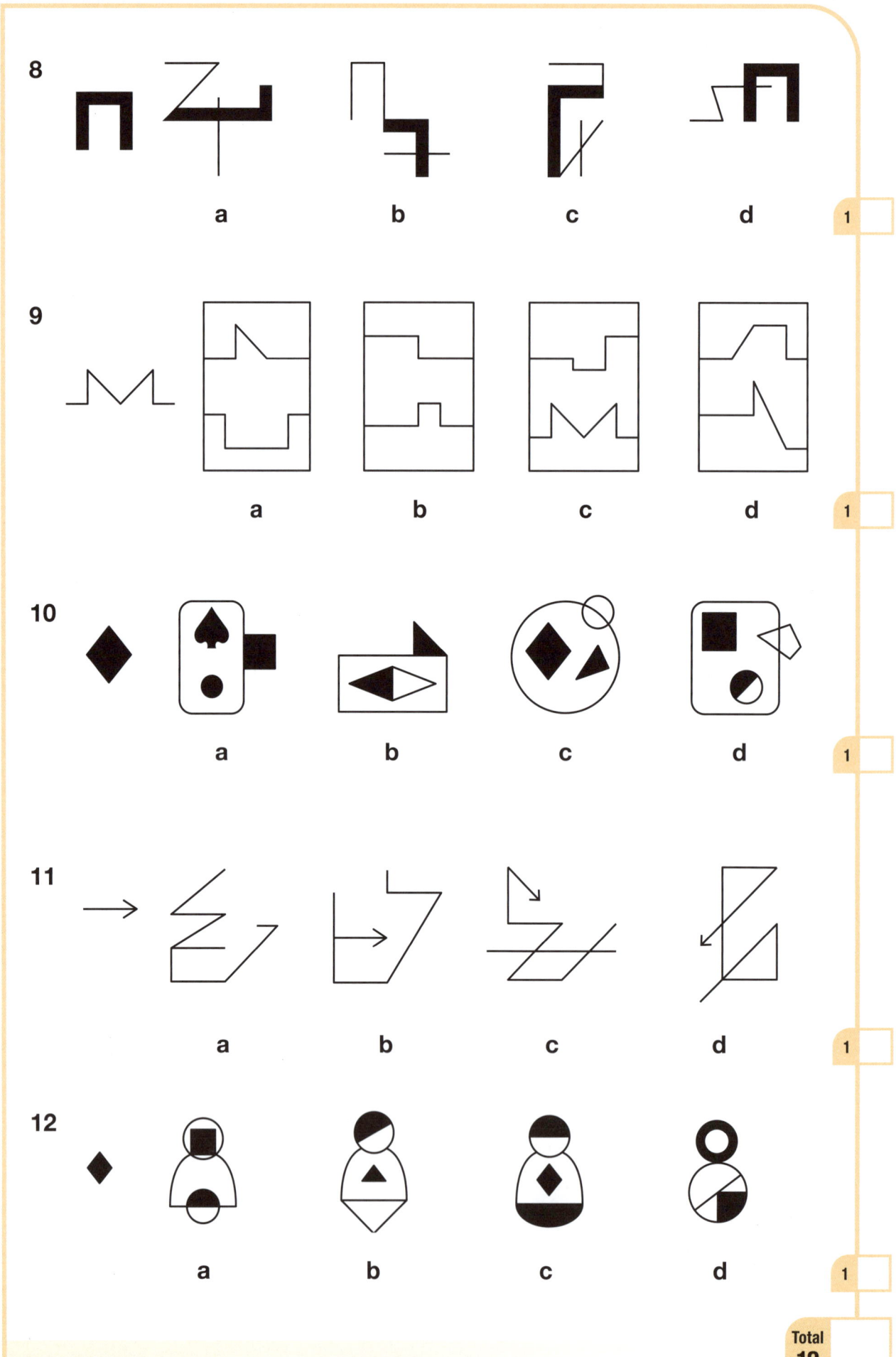

7 Matching Shapes or Reflections

> **KEY SKILL**
>
> These two question types use similar skills. When looking for the matching shape you need to identify the shape that is **exactly the same** as the one that is given. With reflections you are looking for the shape that is the **mirror image** of the shape given, so details will be the same but in a reflected image.

WORKED EXAMPLES

Matching shape

Which one is the same as the one on the left?

1
                    a   b   c   d

Here the picture is of a caterpillar. Start by looking at each part in turn.

The face has two eyes and a smile. Check this with the answer options:
a Option **a** has two eyes and a smile.
b Option **b** has two eyes and a smile.
c Option **c** has two eyes and a smile.
d Option **d** has two eyes but no smile, so cross it out.

The body has five legs. Check this with the answer options left:
a Option **a** only has three legs, so cross it out.
b Option **b** only has four legs which are a different shape, so cross it out.
c Option **c** has five legs, the same as the picture on the left.

So **option c** is the answer.

2
                    a   b   c   d

Here the first picture is a combination of shapes. Look at the different parts in turn. There is a black triangle at the right end. Check this with the answer options:
a Option **a** has a black triangle.
b Option **b** does not have a black triangle, so cross it out.
c Option **c** has a black triangle.
d Option **d** has a black triangle.

> **TOP TIP!**
>
> Remember it is really helpful to cross out an answer option as soon as you work out that it cannot be right.

There is one narrow black bar near the left end. Check this with the options that are left:

a Option **a** has a white band, so cross it out.
c Option **c** has a black band near the left end – a possible answer. Check the final option.
d Option **d** does not have a band across the rectangle, so cross it out.

This leaves **option c** as the answer.

Reflected shape

Which one is a reflection of the one on the left?

In these questions the dotted line represents the mirror, also called the line of reflection. Each part of the shape will be the same distance from the dotted line but reflected on the opposite side.

3

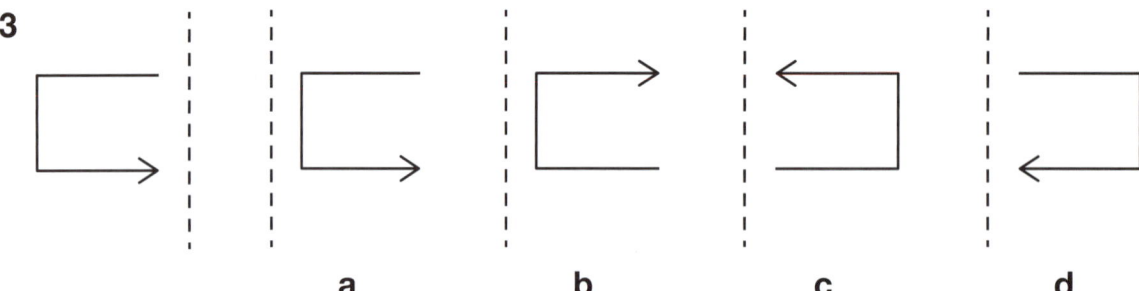

        a   b   c   d

The arrowhead in this shape is close to the mirror line and points to it.
a In option **a**, the arrowhead points away from the mirror line, so cross it out.
b In option **b**, the arrowhead points away from the mirror line, so cross it out.
c In option **c**, the arrowhead points to the line.
d In option **d**, the arrowhead points to the line.

The line ending with the arrowhead is at the bottom of the shape. Check this with the options that are left.
c In option **c**, the arrowhead is at the top, so cross it out.
d In option **d**, the arrowhead is at the bottom.

So **option d** is the correct image because it is a reflection of the shape at the beginning of the line.

Now try these.

Which one on the right is the same as the one on the left?
Circle the letter.

1 a b c d

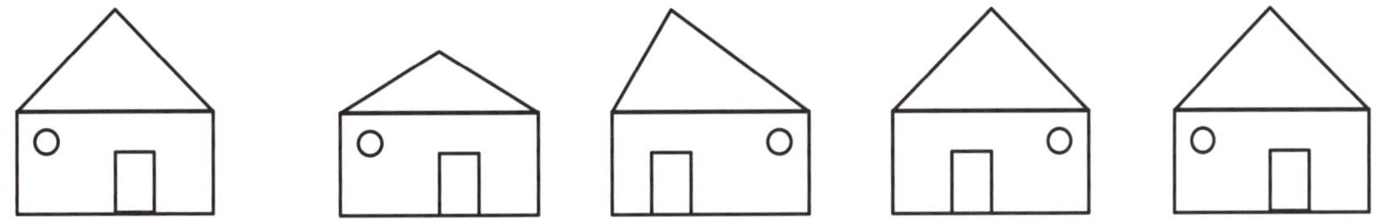

2 a b c d

3 a b c d

4 a b c d

5 a b c d

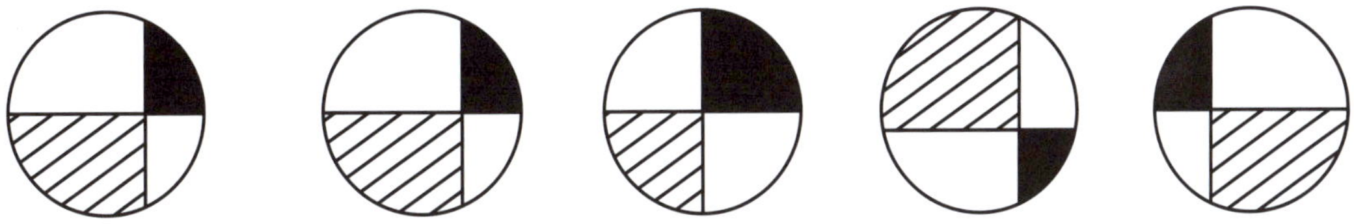

Matching Shapes or Reflections

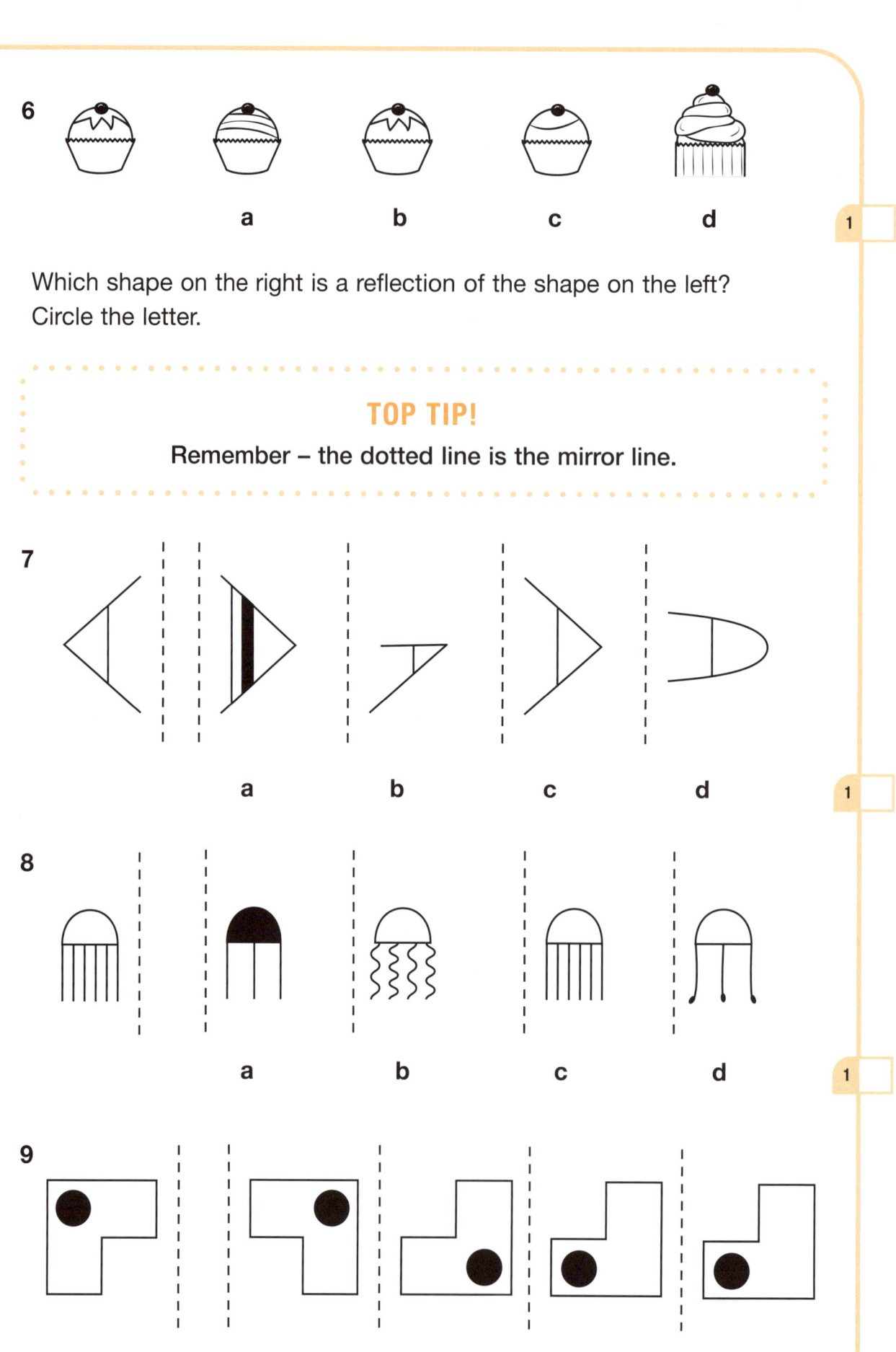

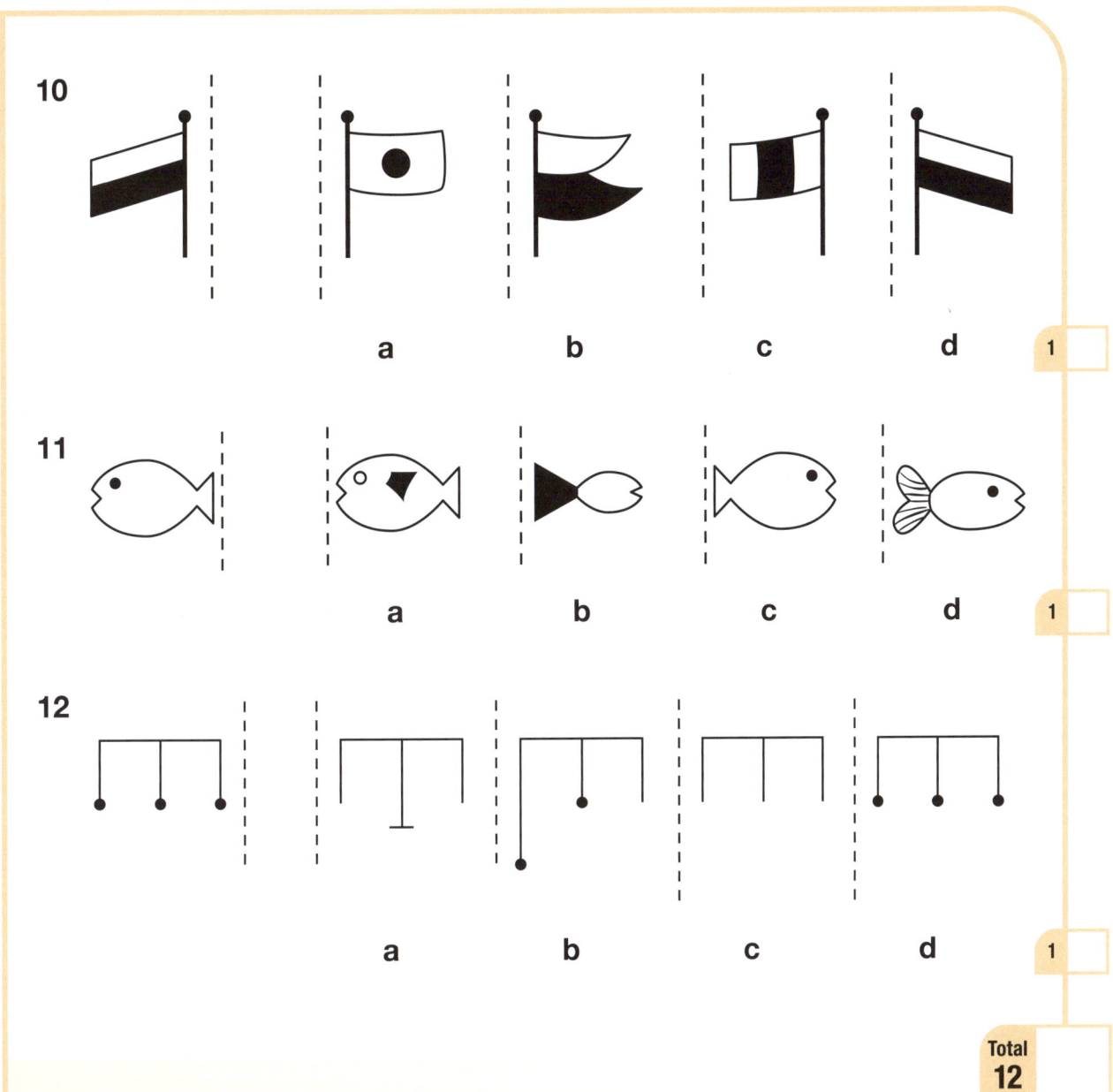

8 Combining Shapes

> **KEY SKILL**
>
> In these questions there are two shapes on the left. You must find the shape on the right that is made up of the two shapes on the left. The correct option will not have any extra lines or shapes in it. Though the original shapes might be turned around they will not be flipped over.
>
> Start by looking at the first of the two shapes on the left and then check to see if it appears in any of the answer options. If it does not appear, cross out the option. Then look carefully at the second shape and see which of the remaining options contains it. The correct answer will have both shapes without any extra lines.

WORKED EXAMPLES

Which shape on the right is made up of the two shapes on the left?

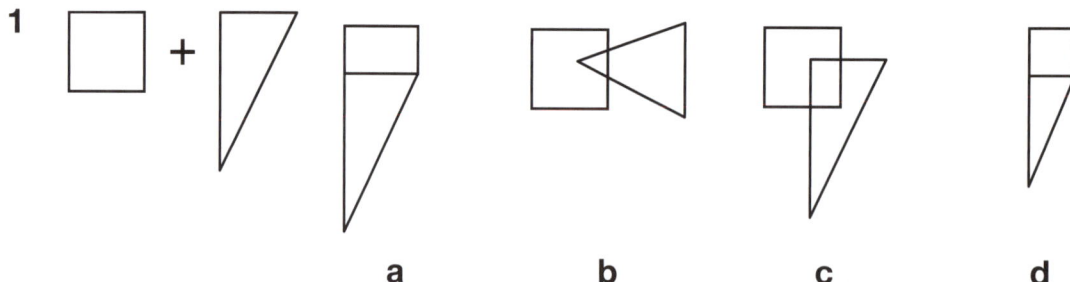

Look at the first shape – it is a square.

Now look at the answer options – do they contain a square of the same size?

a No, it has a small rectangle, so cross out option **a**.
b Yes, option **b** contains a square of the same size.
c Yes, option **c** contains a square of the same size.
d No, the square is smaller, so cross out option **d**.

Now look carefully at the second shape – it is a triangle with a square corner at the top left.

Now look at the options left to consider:
b No, the triangle in option **b** does not have a square corner, so cross it out.
c Yes, option **c** has a triangle with a square corner at the top left.

So **option c** is the answer.

2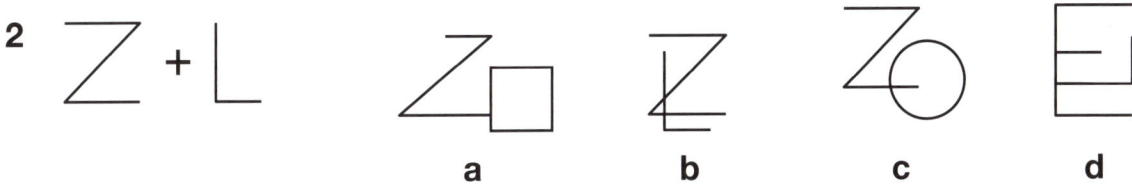

Start by looking at the first shape on the left – it is a Z shape.
Now look at the answer options, do they have a Z shape the same size?

a The top line of the Z shape in option **a** is shorter, so cross it out.
b Yes, option **b** has a Z shape the same size.
c Yes, option **c** has a Z shape the same size.
d There is no Z shape in option **d**, so cross it out.

Look at the second shape – it is an L shape.
Now check the remaining answer options:
b Yes, option **b** has an L shape.
c There is no L shape in option **c**, so cross it out.

This gives **option b** as the answer.

Now try these.

Combining Shapes

Which shape on the right is made up of the two shapes on the left? Circle the letter.

1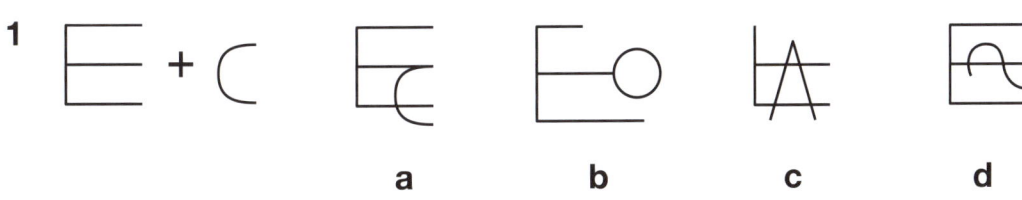

2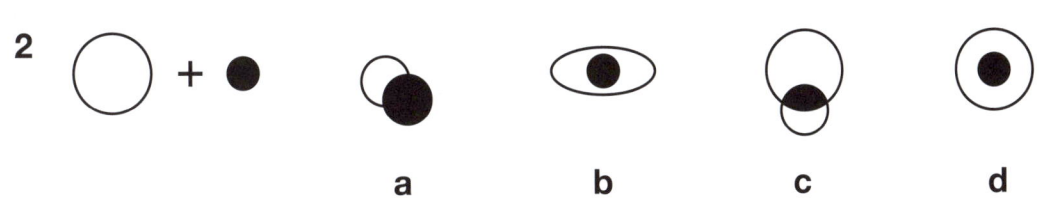

3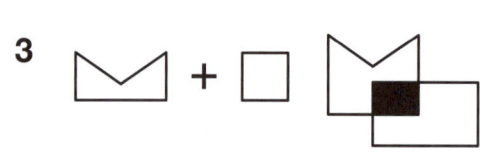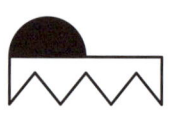
   a b c d

4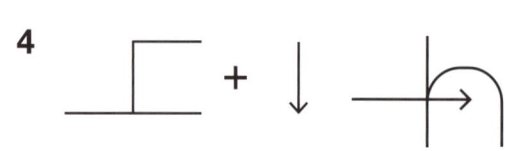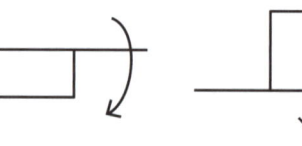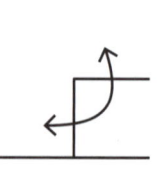
   a b c d

5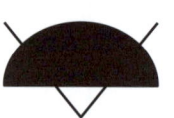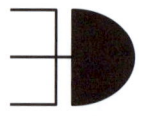
   a b
   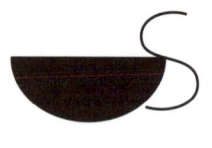 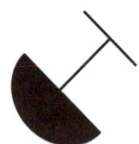
   c d

6
   a b c d

7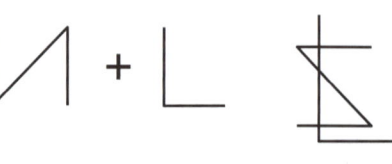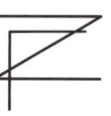
   a b c d

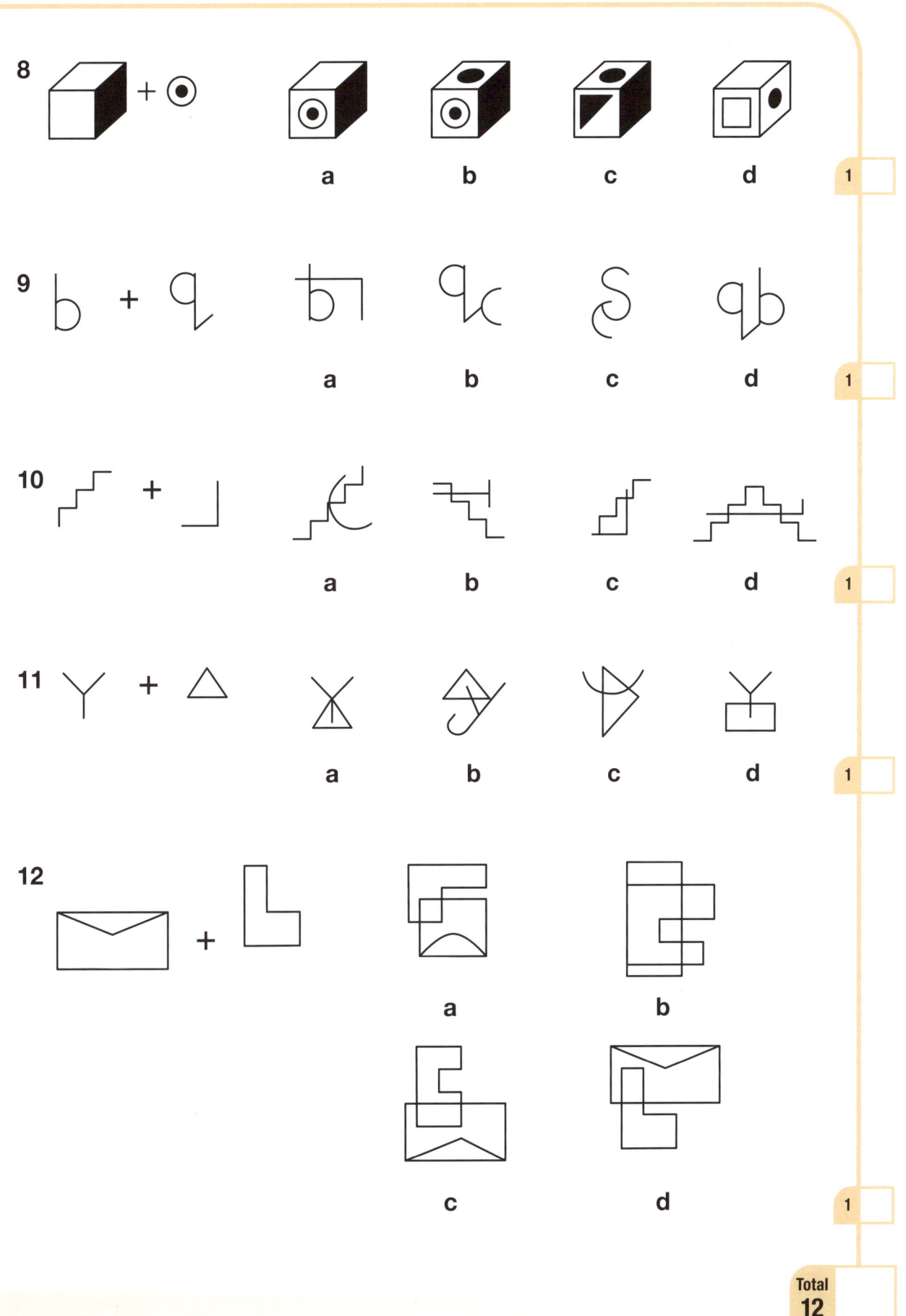

Puzzle 1

All 26 letters of the alphabet are hidden in this pattern.
Can you find them?

A B C D E F G H I J K L M N O P Q R S T U V W X Y Z

Mixed Papers

Mixed Paper 1

Which is the odd one out? Circle the letter.

1 a b c d

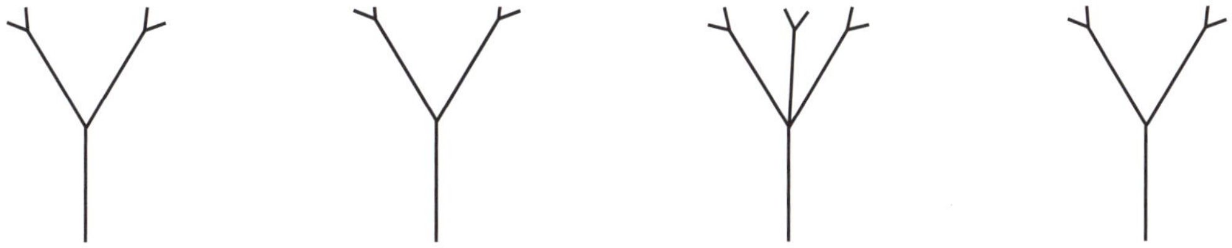

2 a b c d

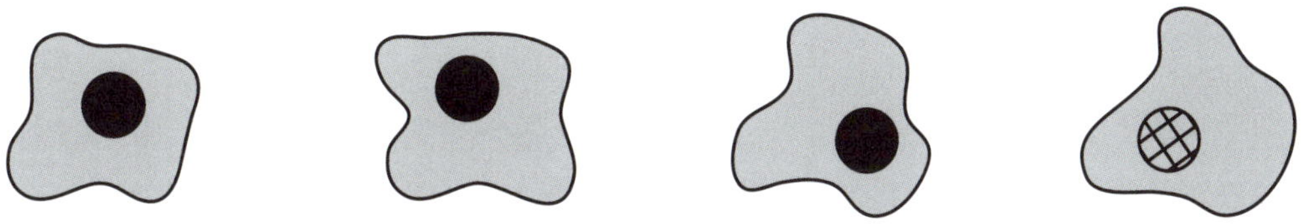

3 a b c d

4 a b c d

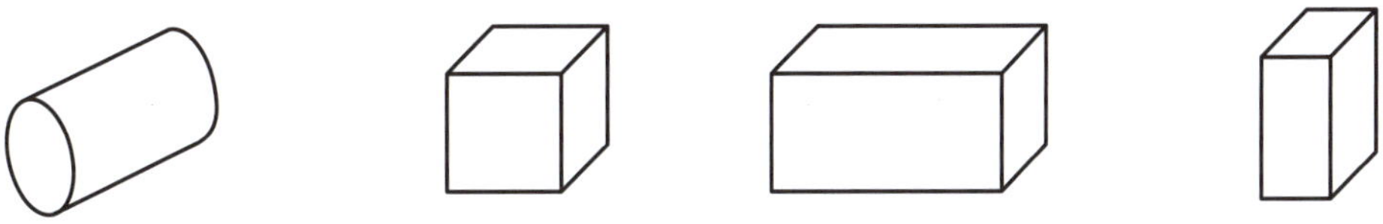

5 a b c d

Which shape on the right is made from the two shapes on the left? Circle the letter.

6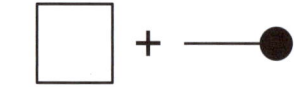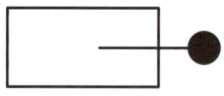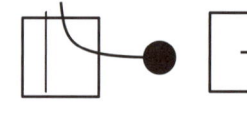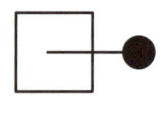
                            a   **b**   **c**   **d**

7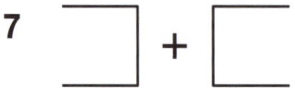
                            a   **b**   **c**   **d**

8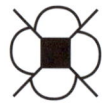
                            a   **b**   **c**   **d**

9
                            a   **b**   **c**   **d**

10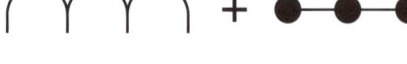

      a   **b**   **c**   **d**

Which shape on the right belongs to the group on the left? Circle the letter.

11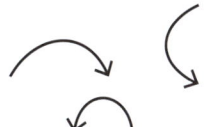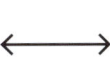

                         a   b   c   d

12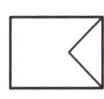

                         a   b   c   d

13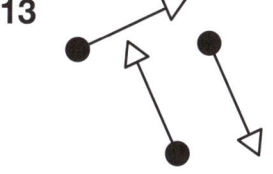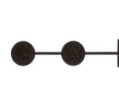

                         a   b   c   d

14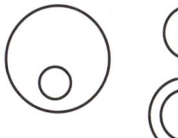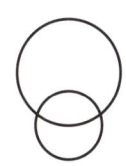

                         a   b   c   d

15

                         a   b   c   d

Mixed Paper 1

Which one completes the second pair in the same way as the first pair? Circle the letter.

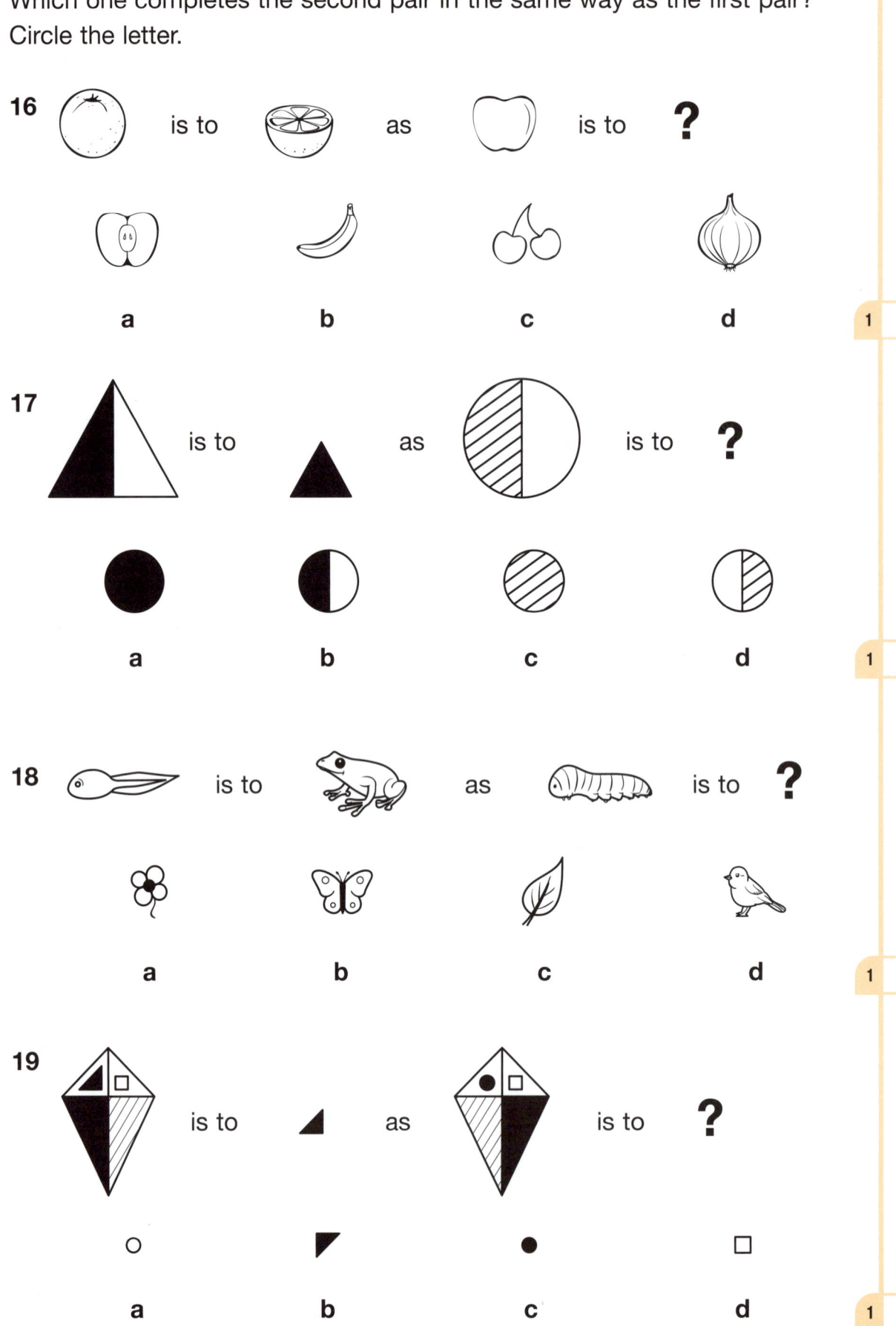

20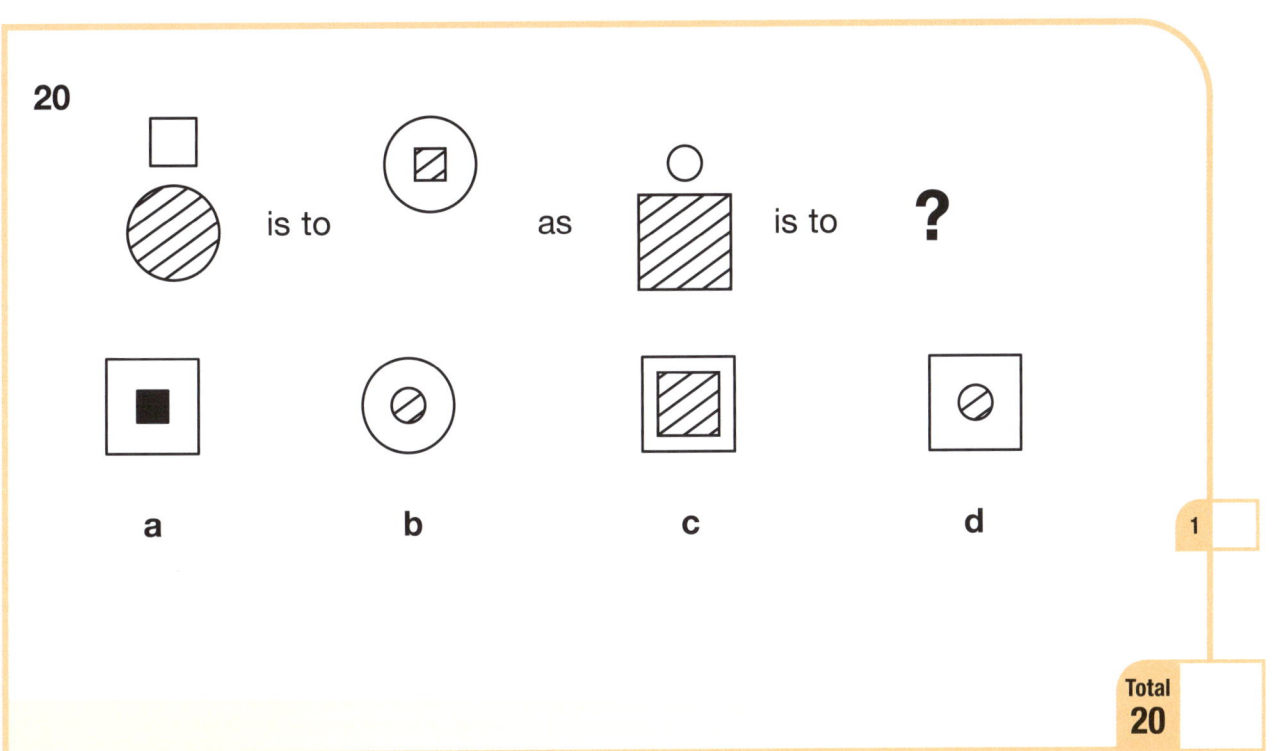

Mixed Paper 2

Which one comes next? Circle the letter.

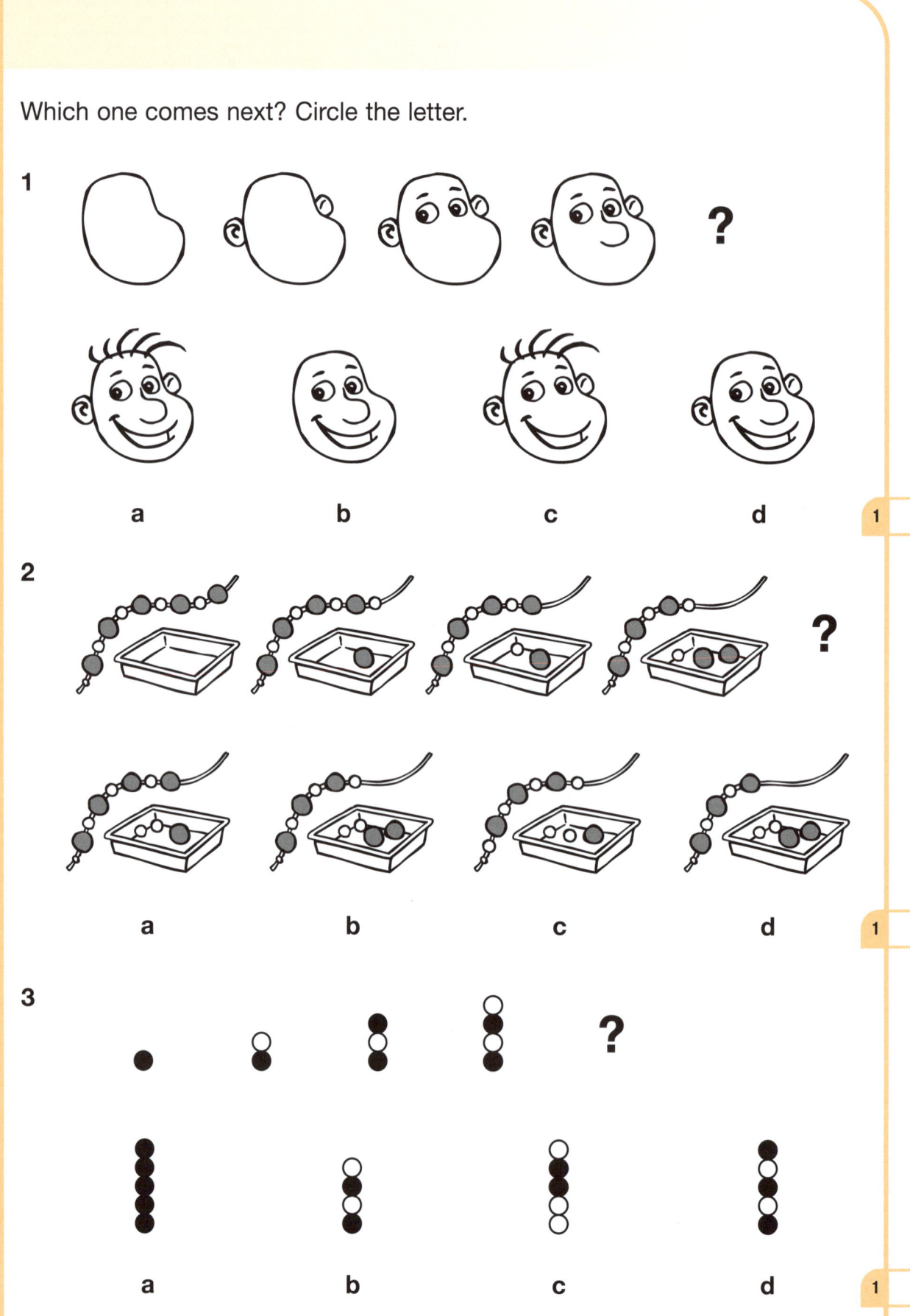

4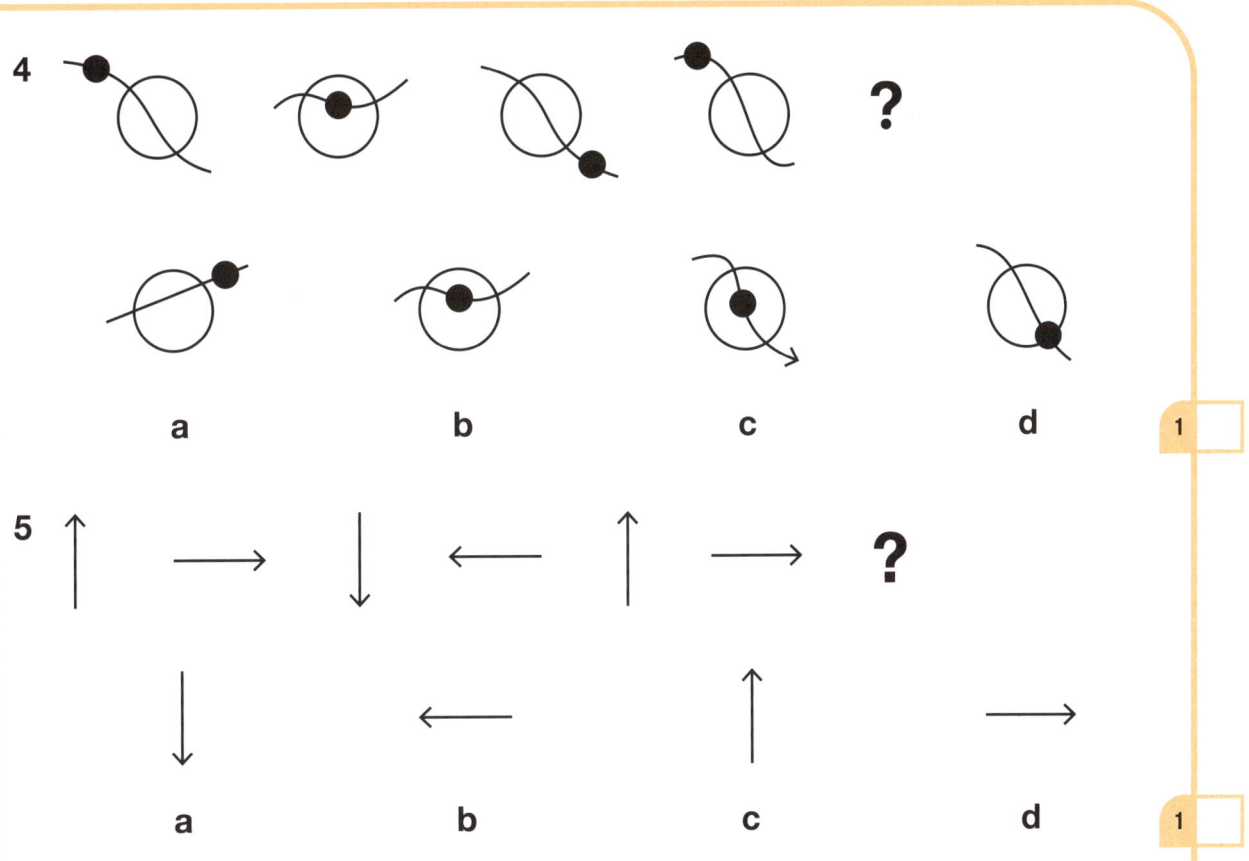

5

Which one on the right belongs to the group on the left? Circle the letter.

6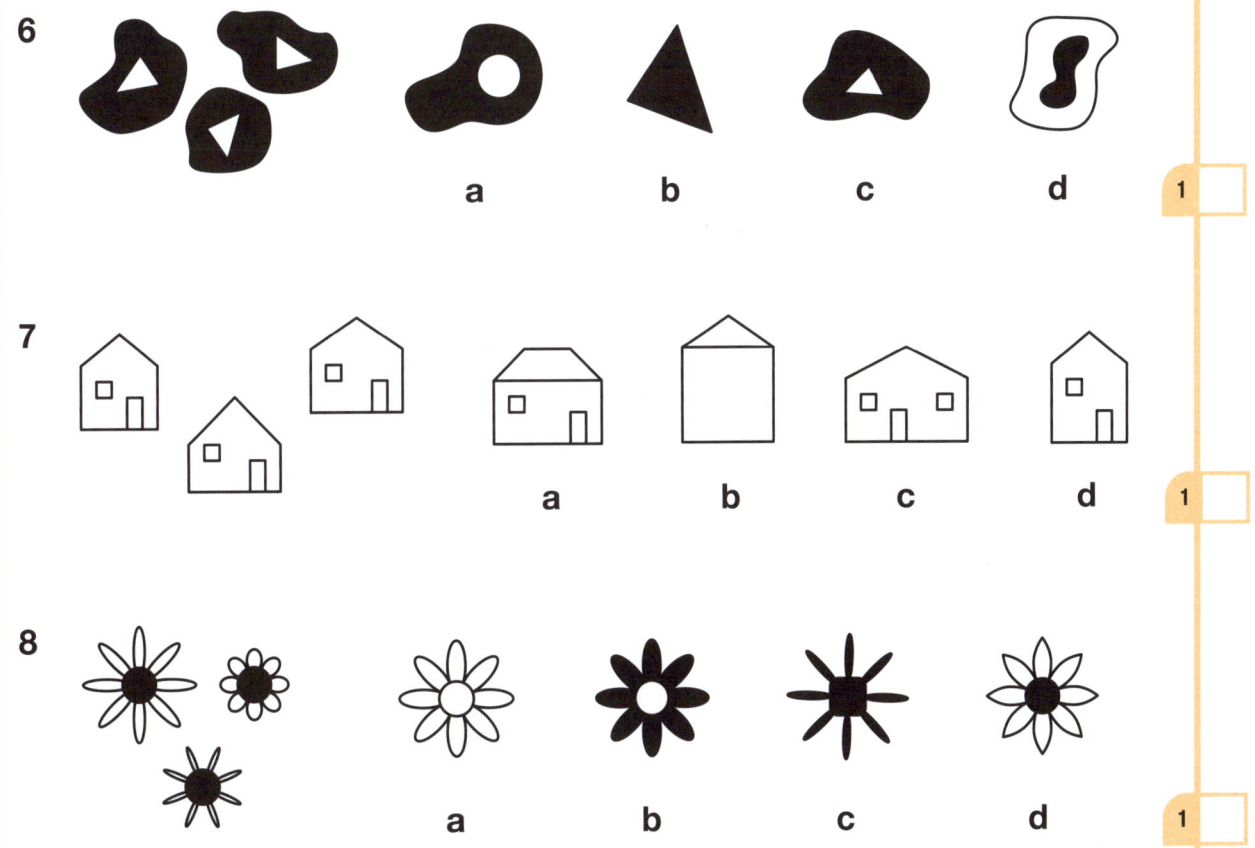

7

8

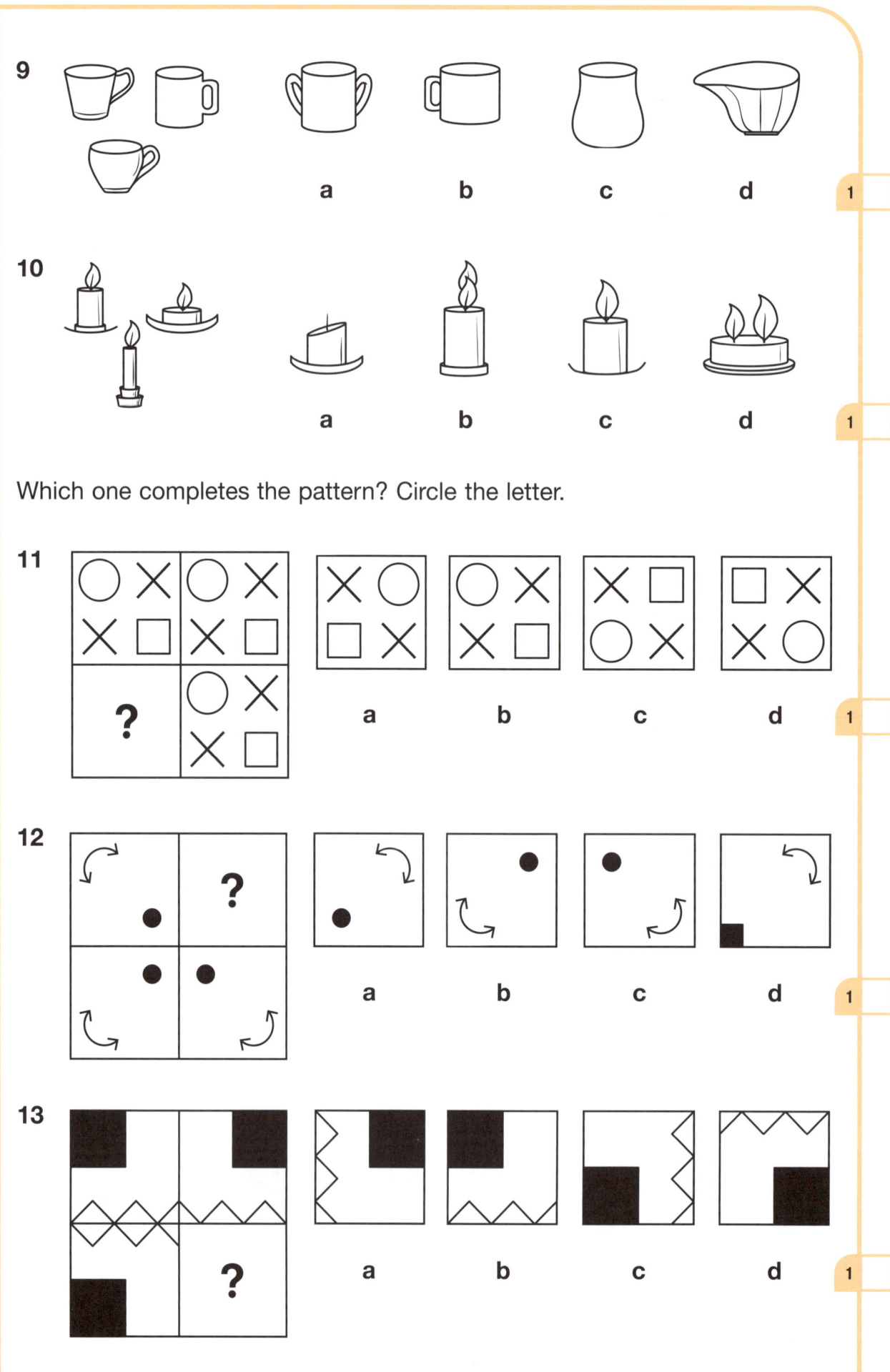

Which one completes the pattern? Circle the letter.

14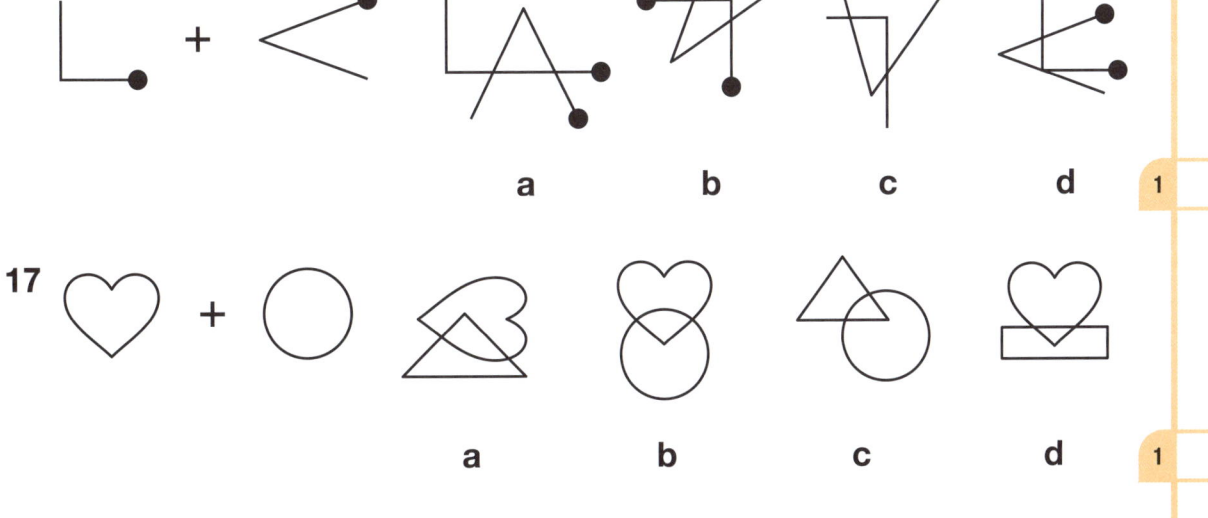

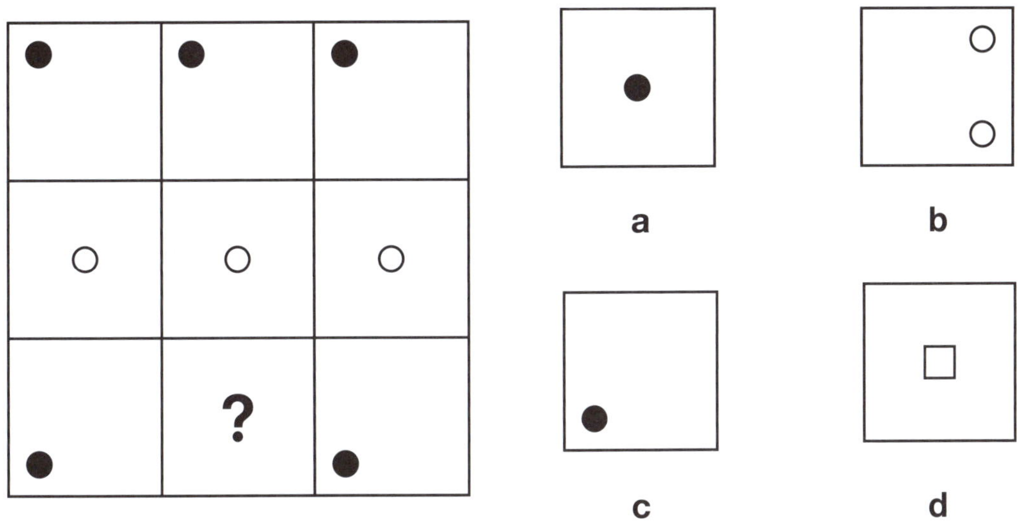

15

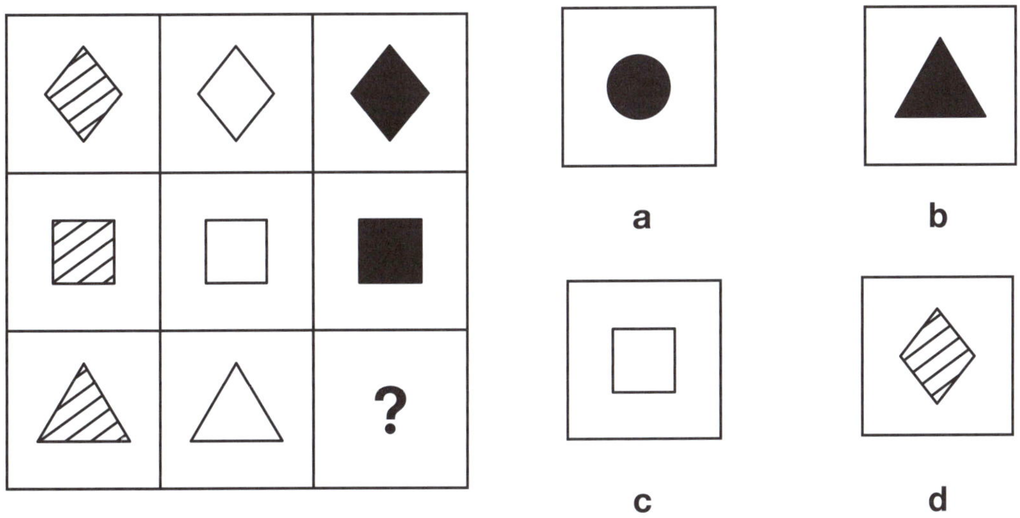

Which shape on the right is made up of the two shapes on the left? Circle the letter.

16

17

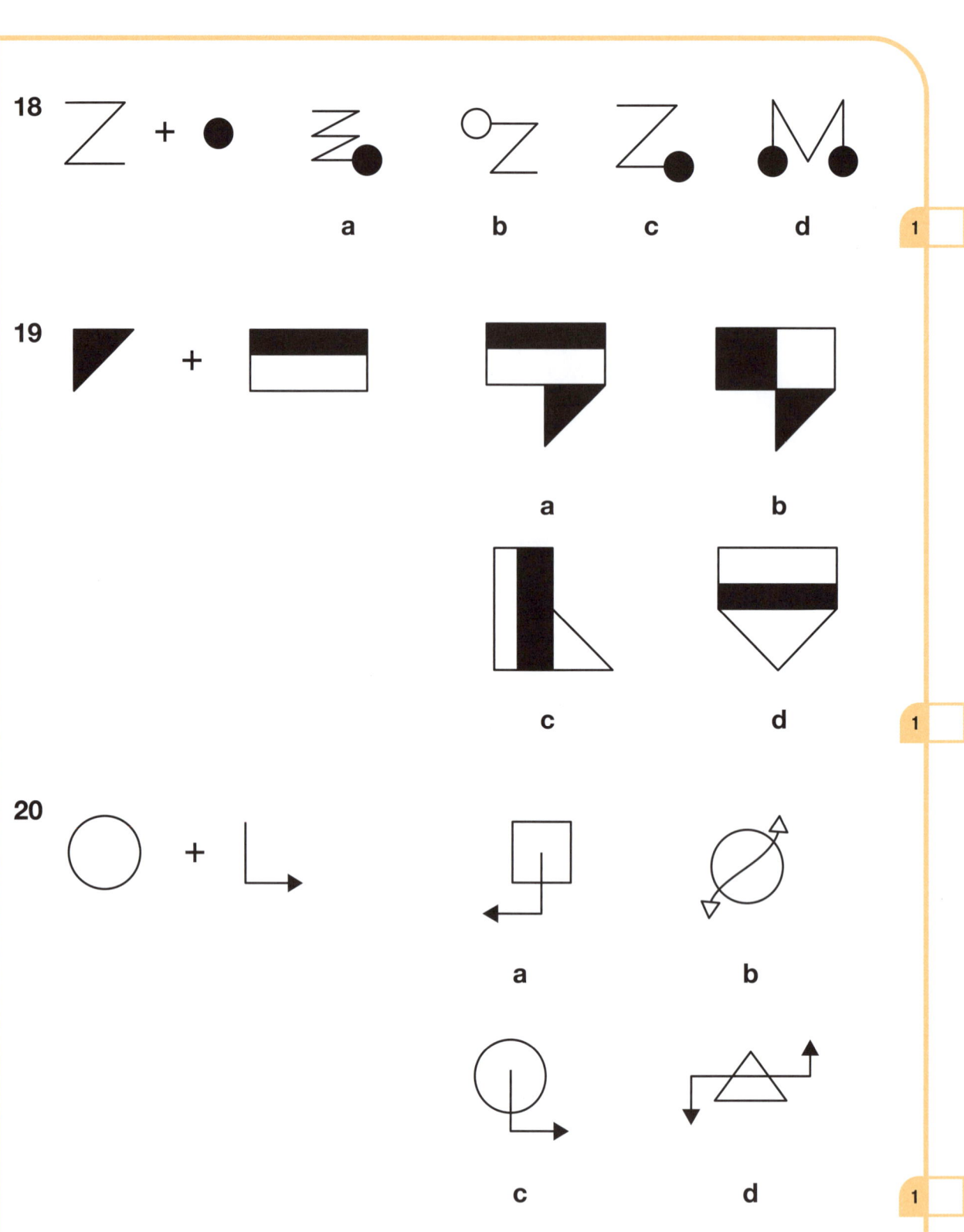

Mixed Paper 3

In which shape on the right is the shape on the left hidden? Circle the letter.

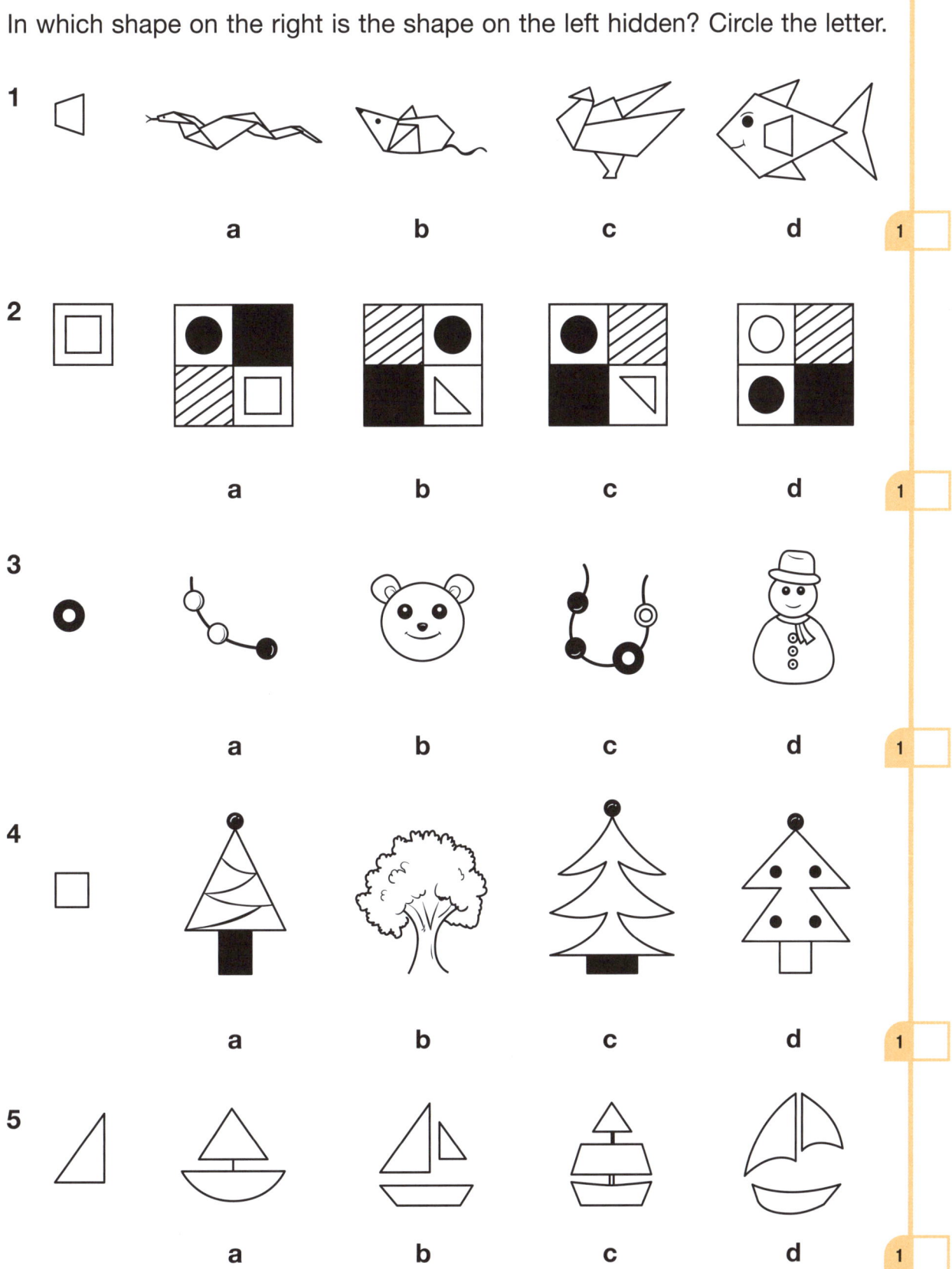

Which one matches the shape on the left? Circle the letter.

6
                    a   b   c   d

7
                    a   b   c   d

8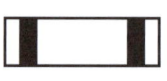
                    a   b   c   d

9
                    a   b   c   d

10
                    a   b   c   d

Which one completes the second pair in the same way as the first pair? Circle the letter.

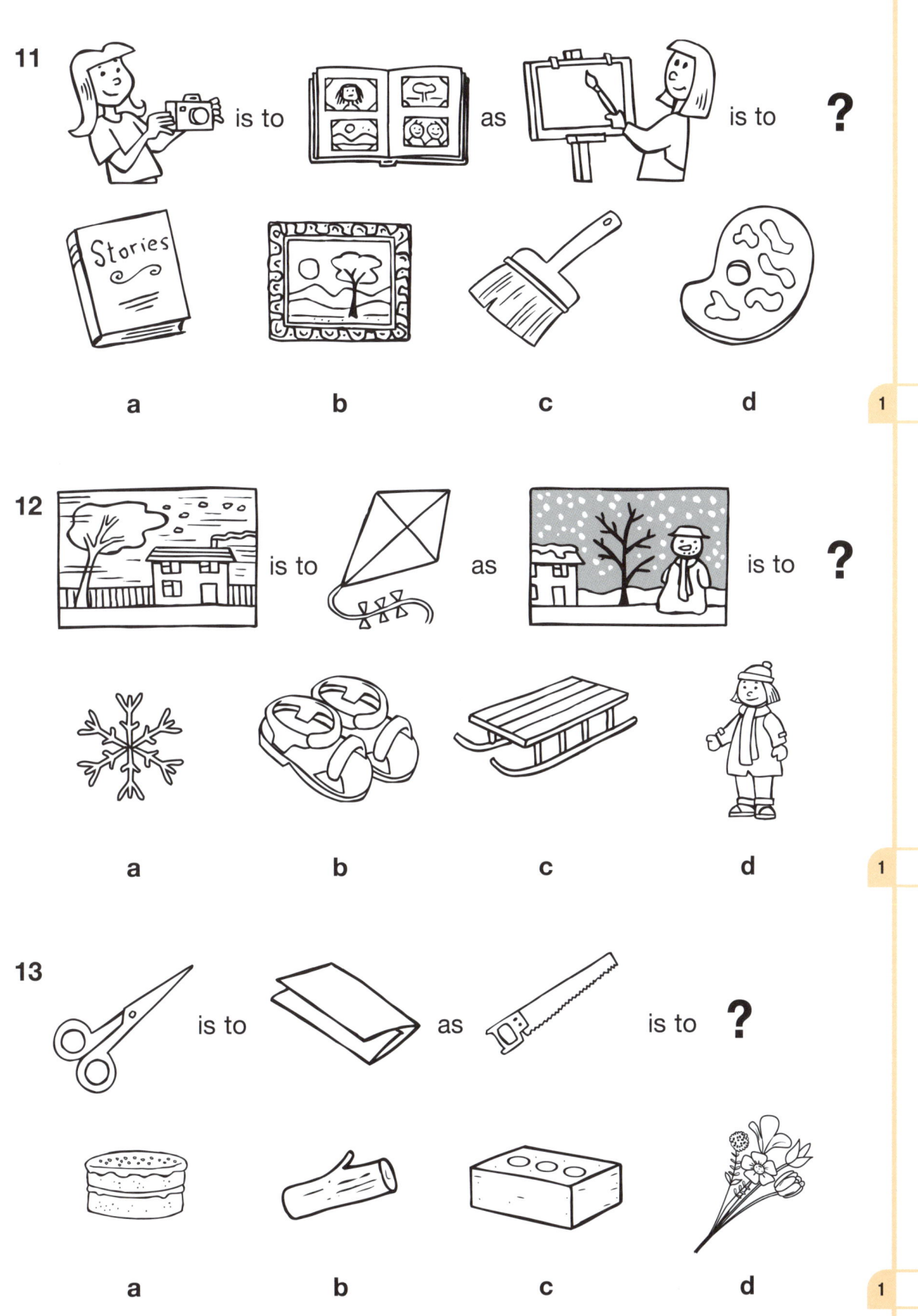

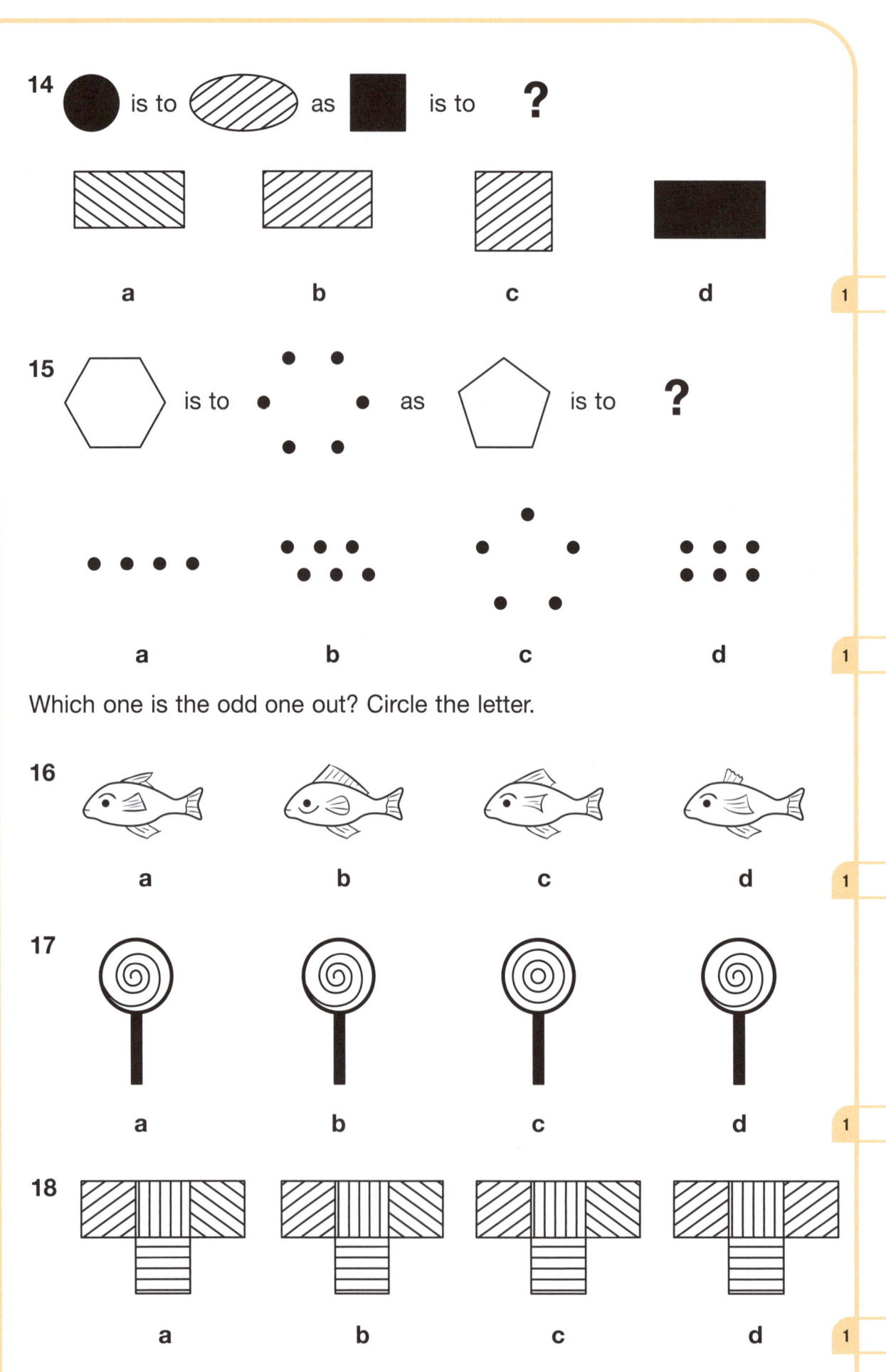

19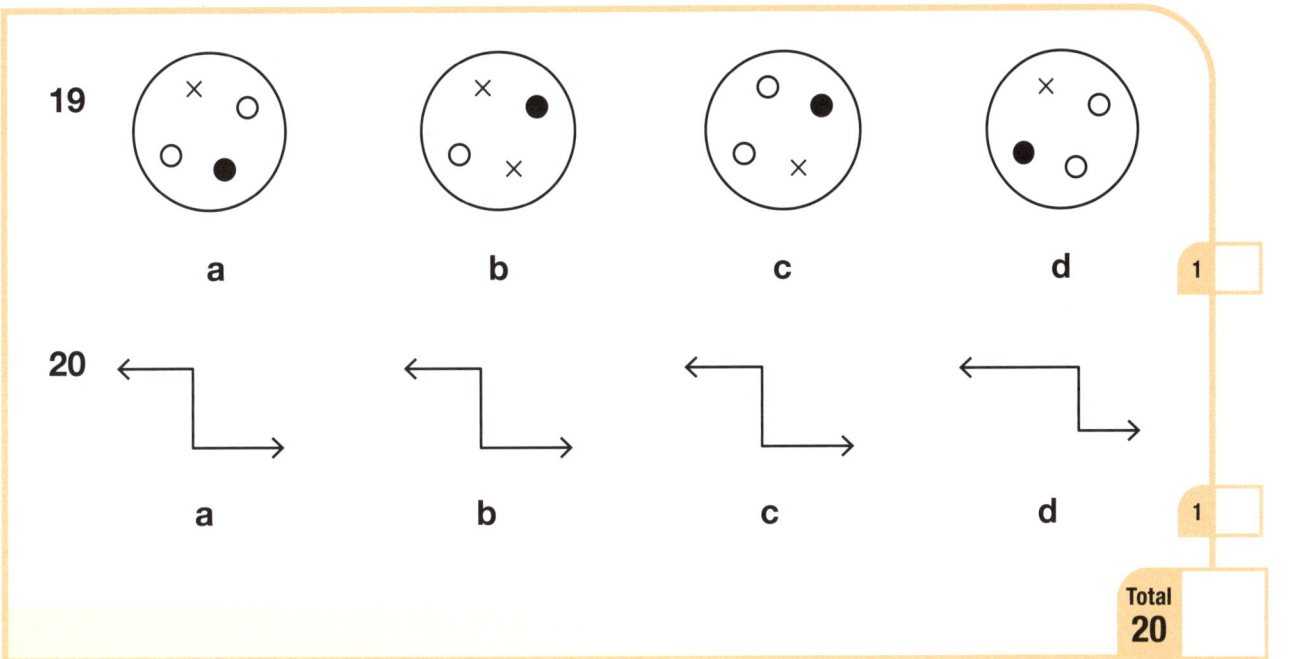

Mixed Paper 4

Which one on the right belongs to the group on the left? Circle the letter.

1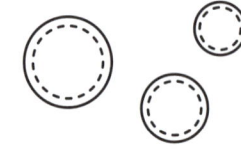
                               a   b   c   d

2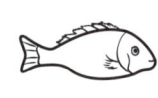
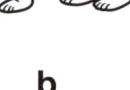
                               a   b   c   d

3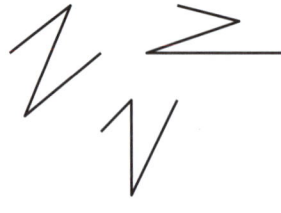
                               a   b   c   d

4
                               a   b   c   d

5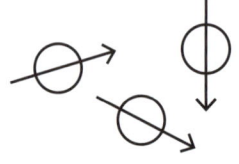
                               a   b   c   d

Which one comes next? Circle the letter.

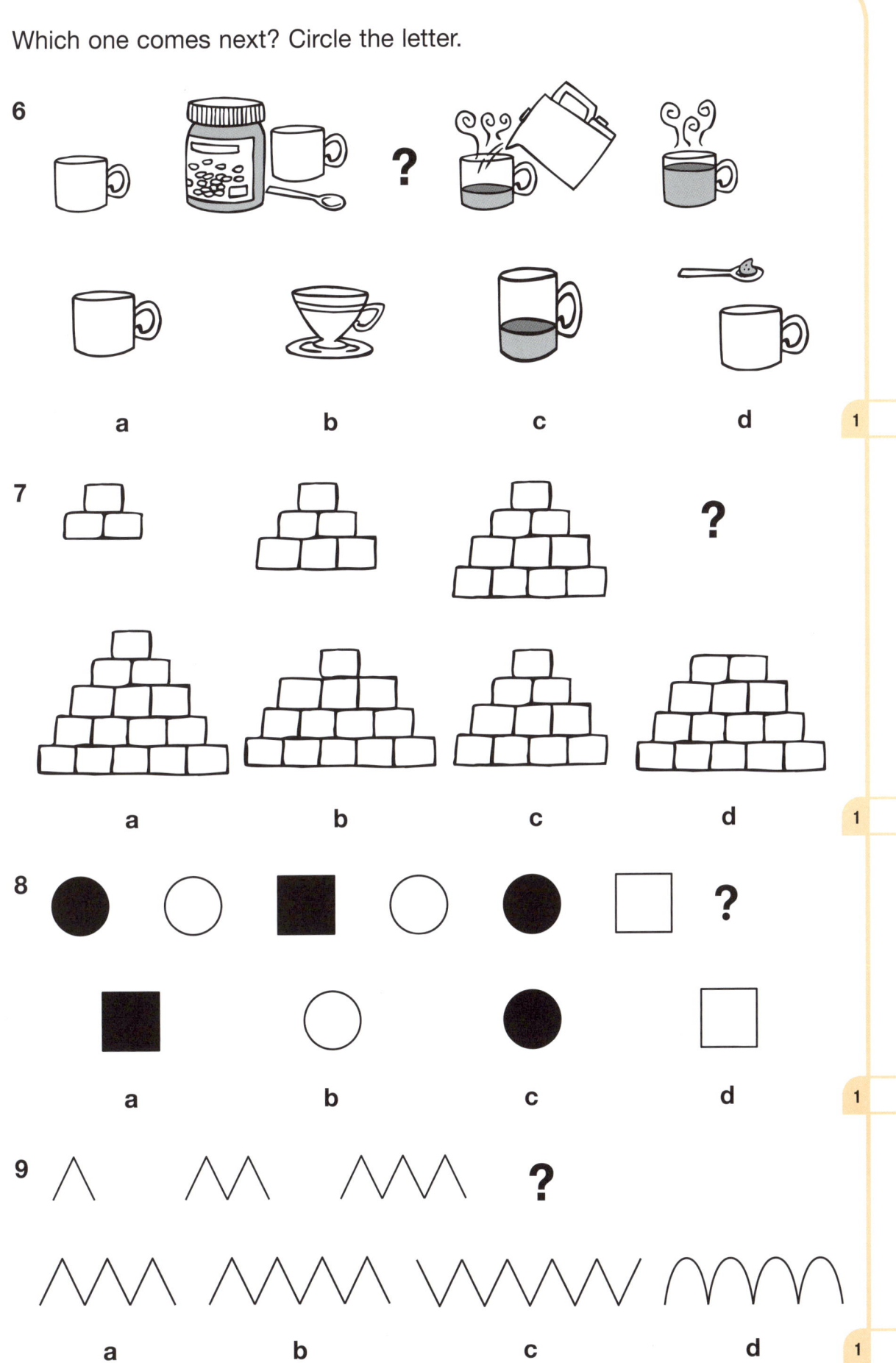

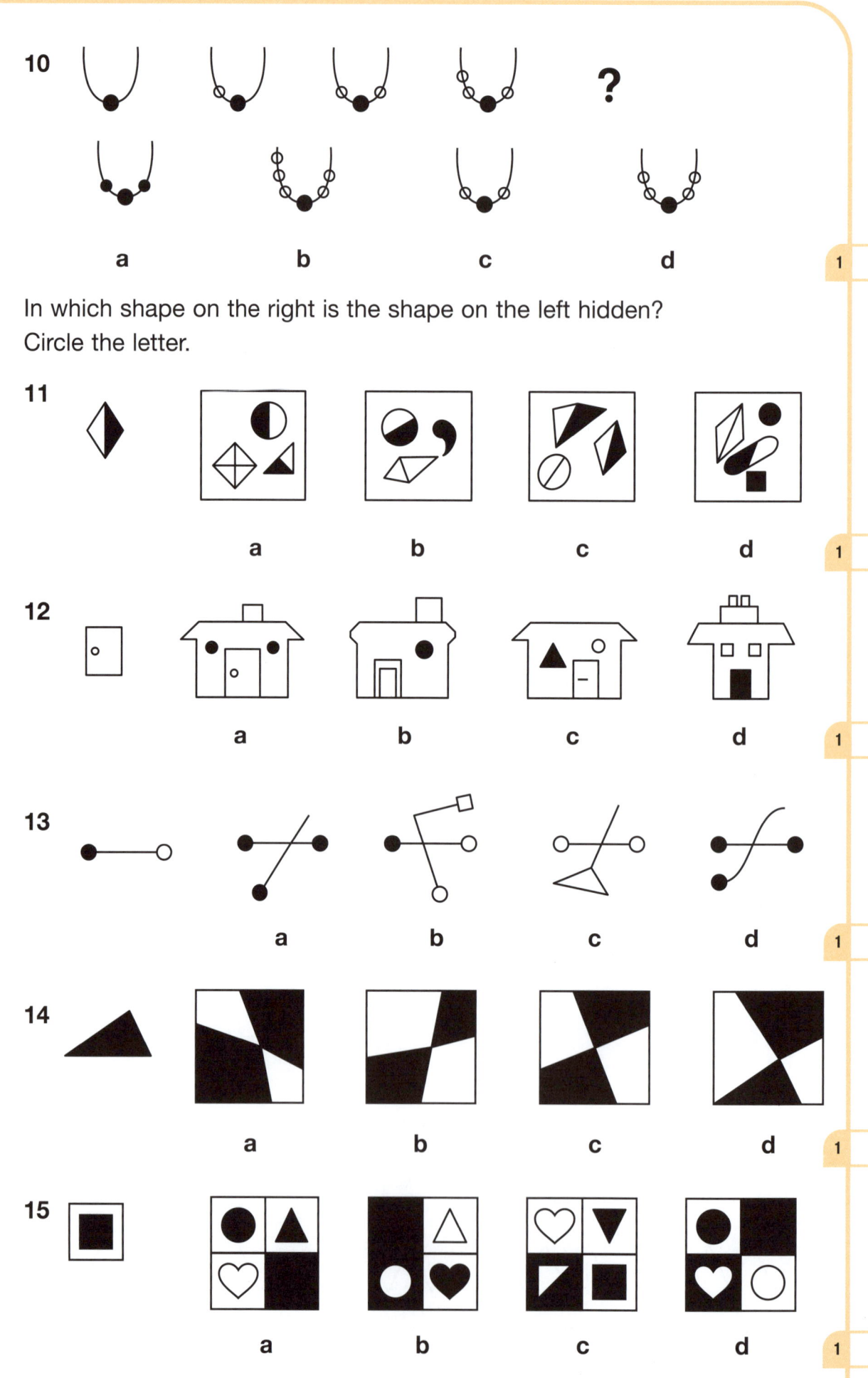

Which one completes the pattern? Circle the letter.

16   a   b   c   d

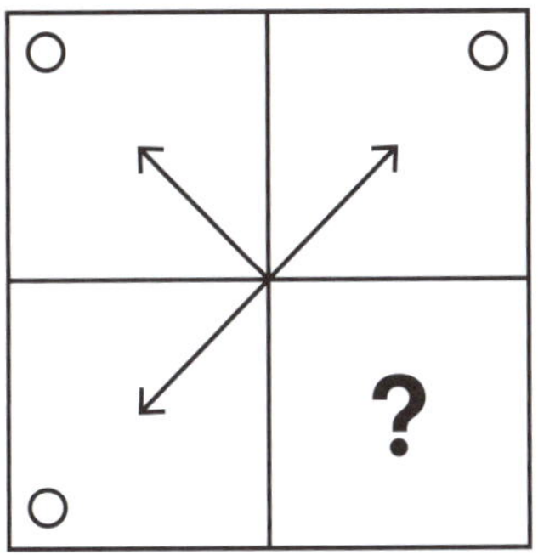

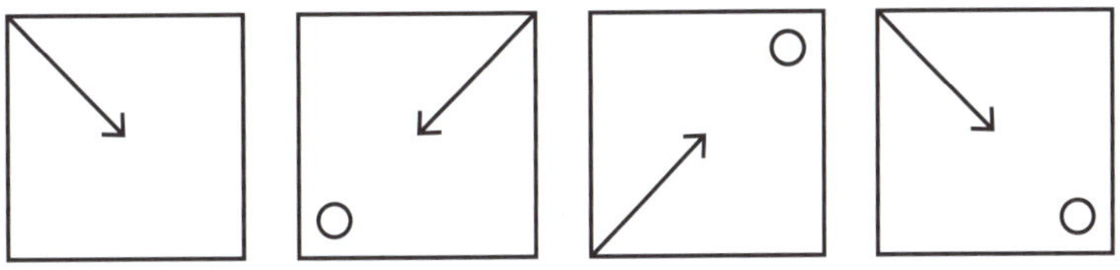

17   a   b   c   d

18   a   b   c   d

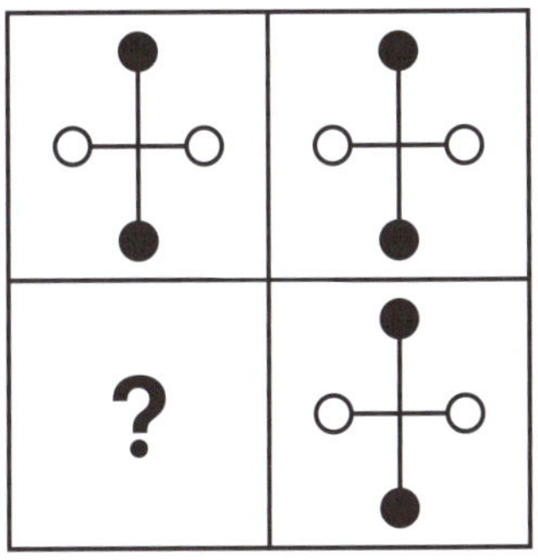

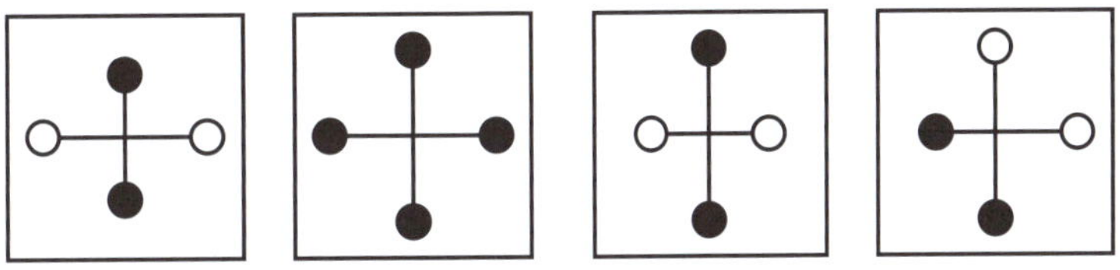

19   a   b   c   d

20   a   b   c   d

Mixed Paper 4

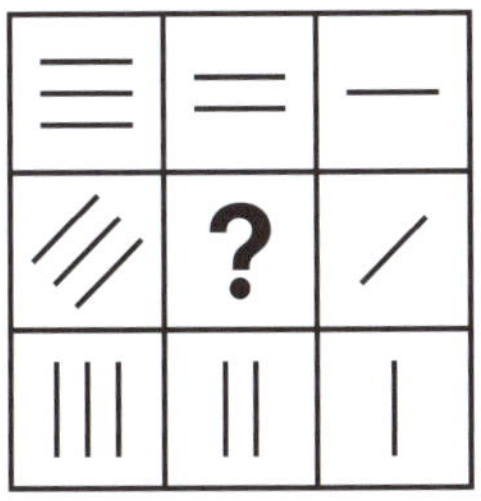

Total **20**

Mixed Paper 5

Which one is the odd one out? Circle the letter.

1

    a   b   c   d

2

    a   b   c   d

3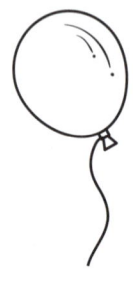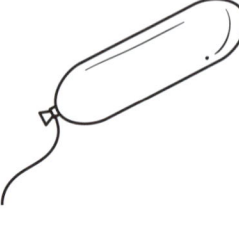

    a   b   c   d

4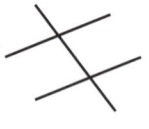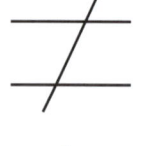

    a   b   c   d

5

    a   b   c   d

Which one on the right belongs to the group on the left? Circle the letter.

6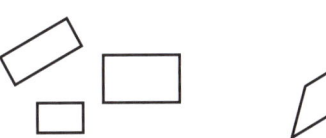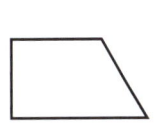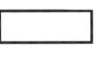

                a   b   c   d

7 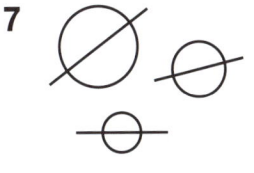   a   b   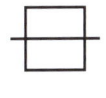

                a   b   c   d

8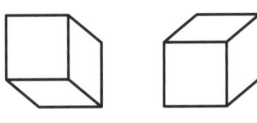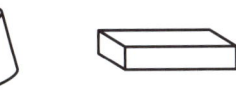

                a   b   c   d

9 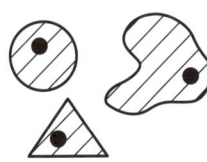   a      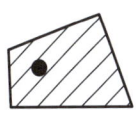   

                a   b   c   d

10    a         

                a   b   c   d

Mixed Paper 5

Which one completes the second pair in the same way as the first pair? Circle the letter.

11 is to as is to **?**

a **b** **c** **d**

1

12 is to as is to **?**

a **b** **c** **d**

1

13 is to as is to **?**

a **b** **c** **d**

1

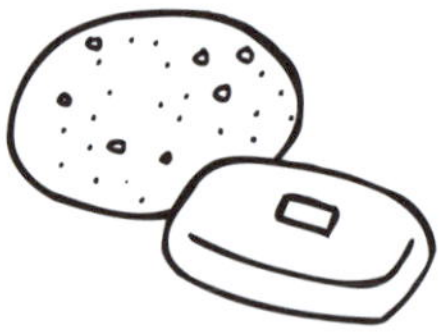

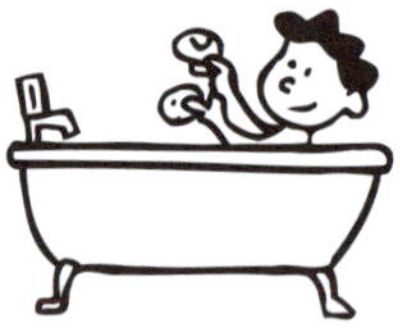

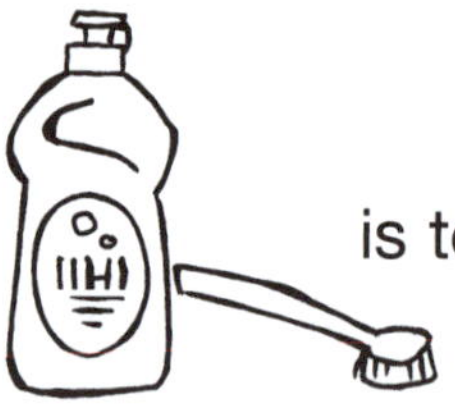

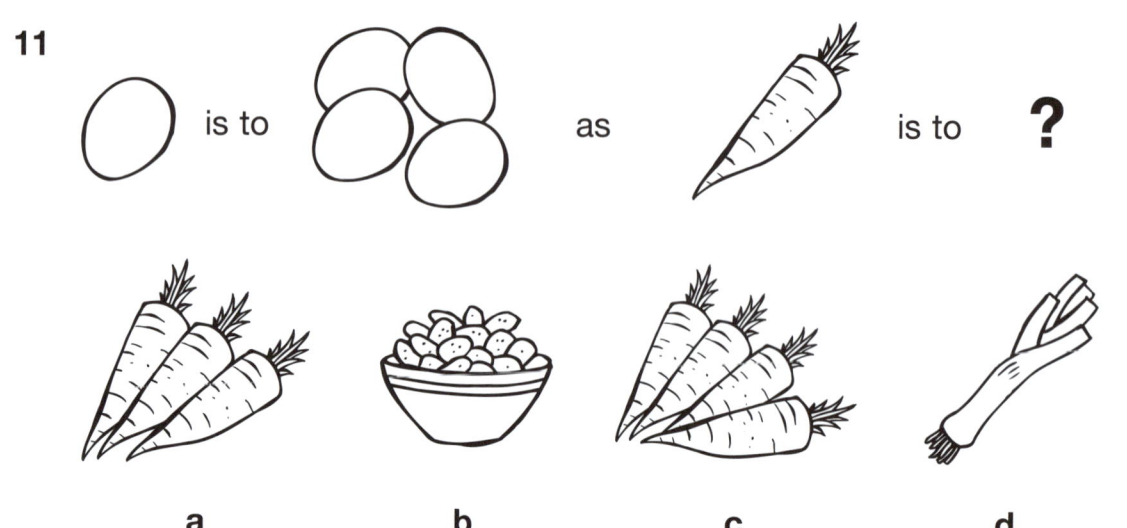

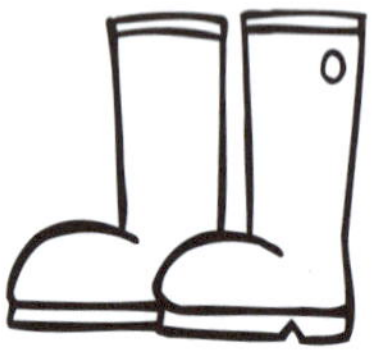

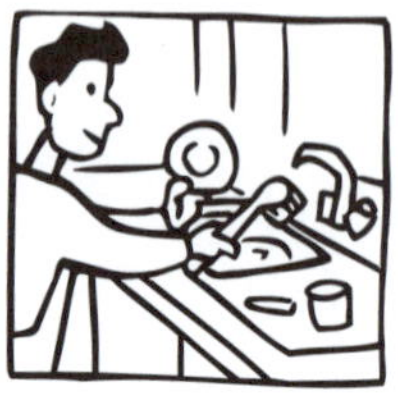

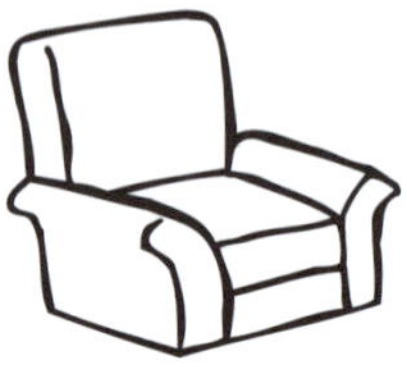

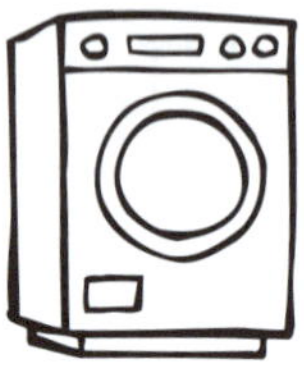

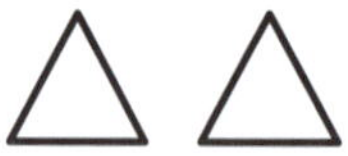

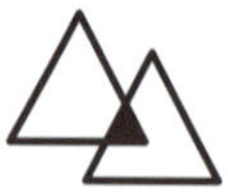

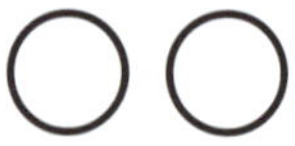

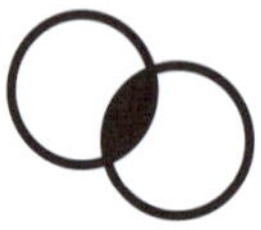

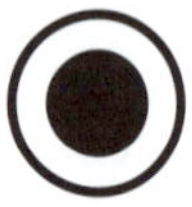

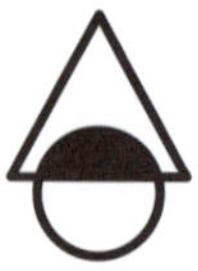

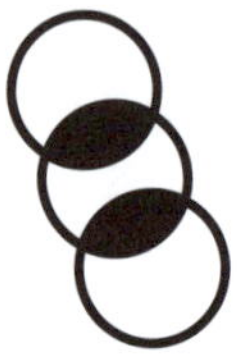

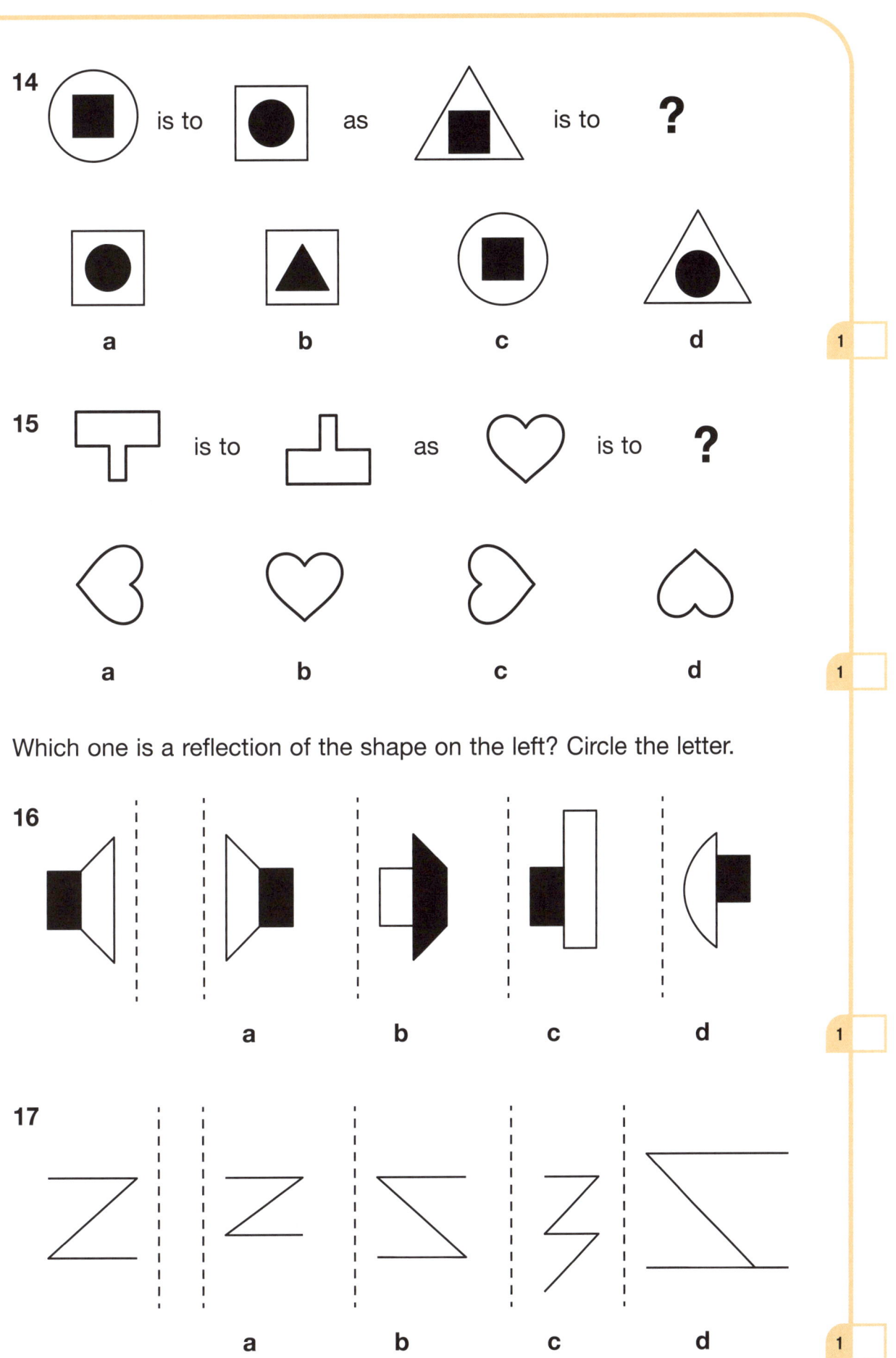

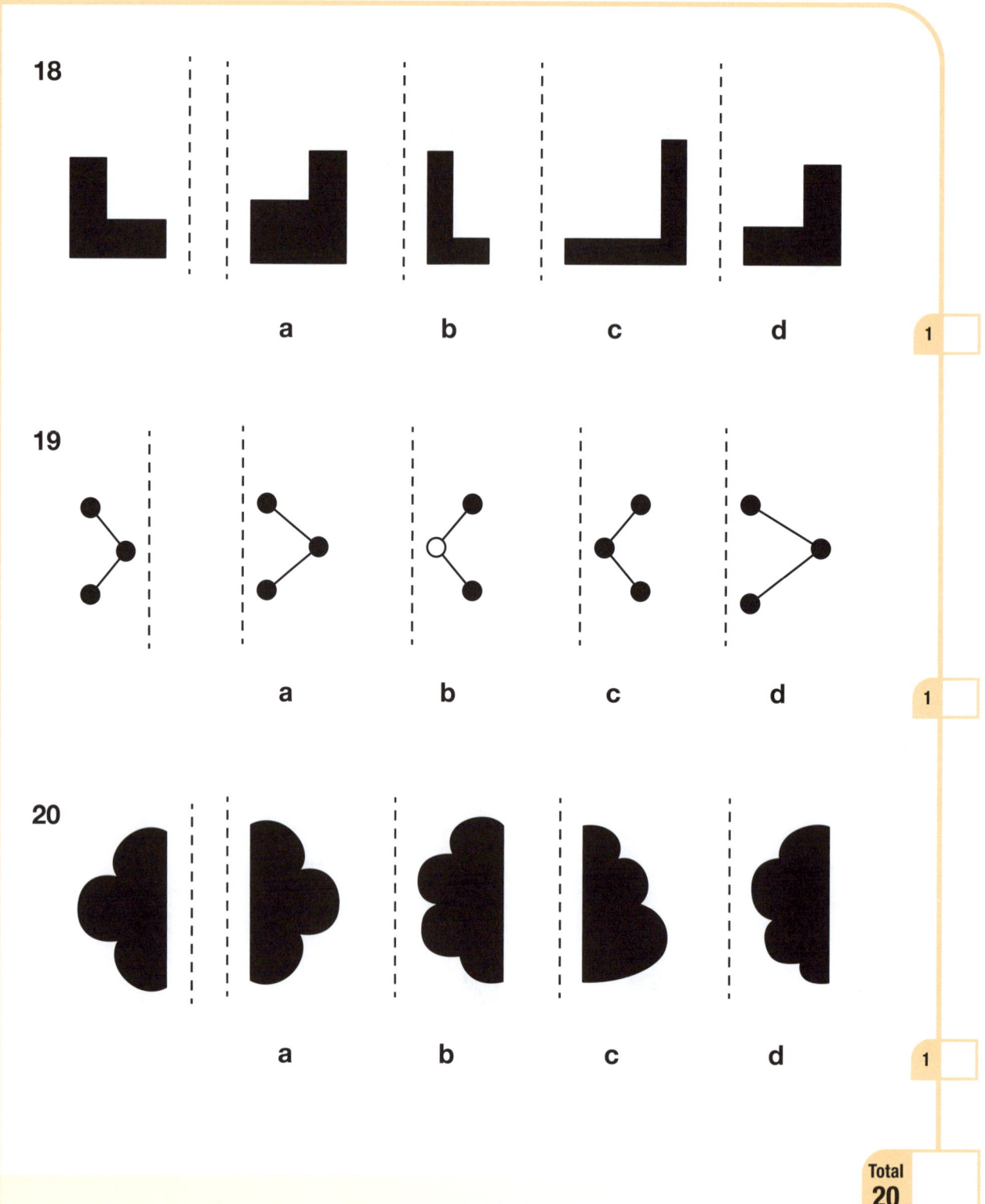

Mixed Paper 6

Which one completes the pattern? Circle the letter.

1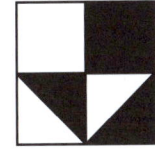
                                  a   b   c   d

2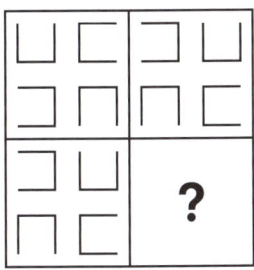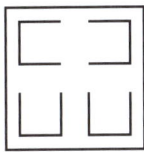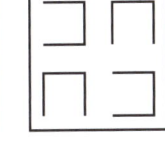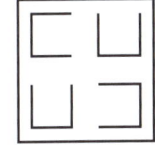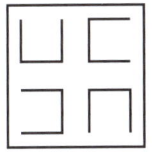
                                  a   b   c   d

3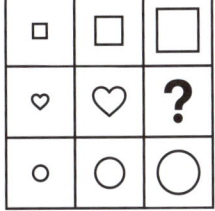
                                  a   b   c   d

4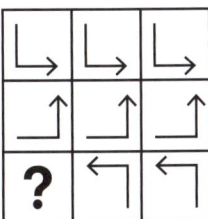
                                  a   b   c   d

5
                                  a   b   c   d

Which one comes next? Circle the letter.

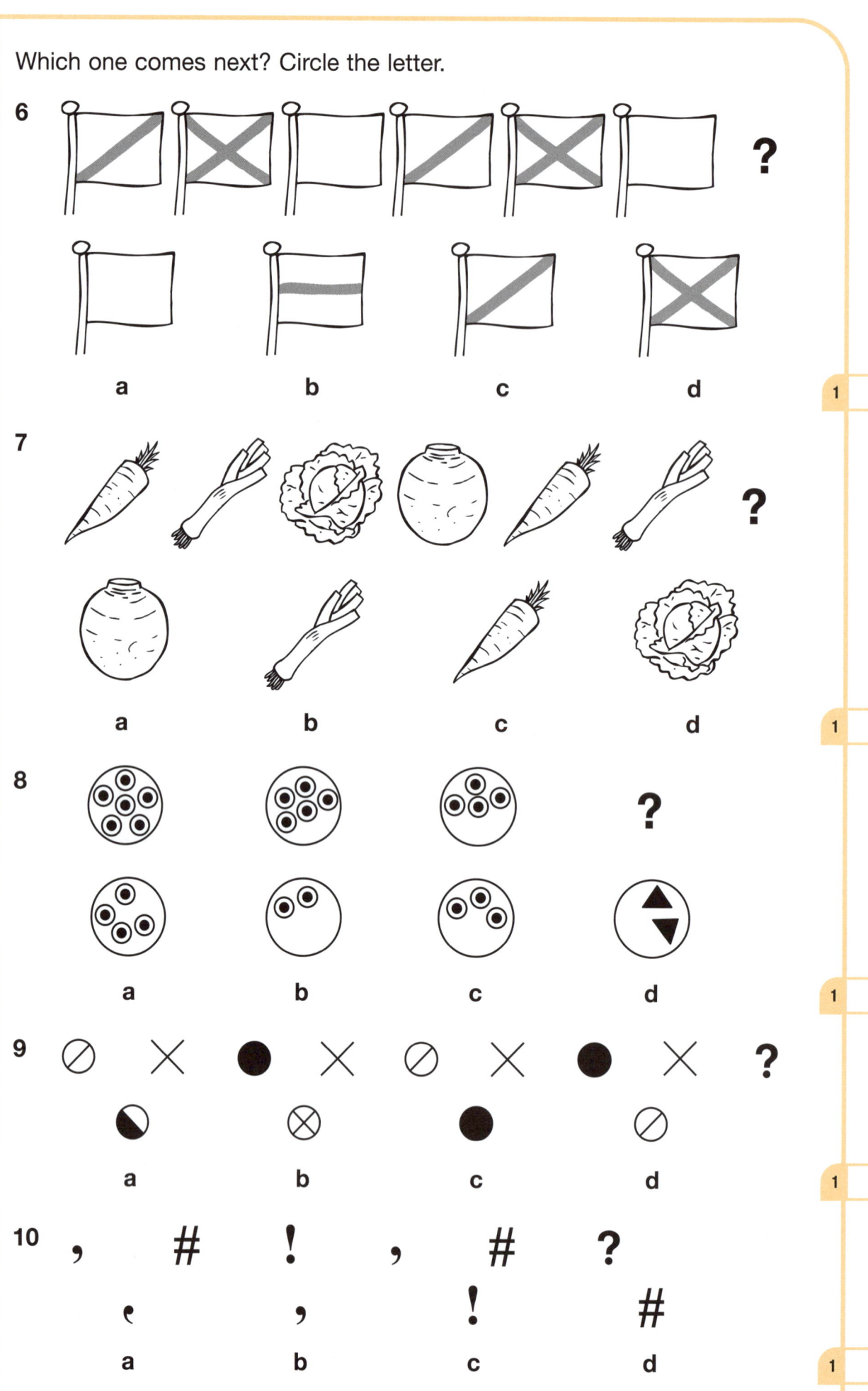

Which shape on the right is made from the two shapes on the left? Circle the letter.

11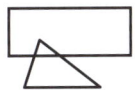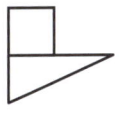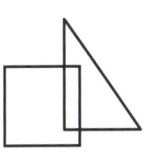
                        a   b   c   d

12
                        a   b   c   d

13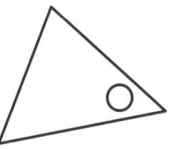
                        a   b   c   d

14
                        a   b   c   d

15
                        a   b   c   d

Mixed Paper 6

Which one is the odd one out? Circle the letter.

Mixed Paper 7

Which one on the right belongs to the group on the left? Circle the letter.

1.   a   b   c   d

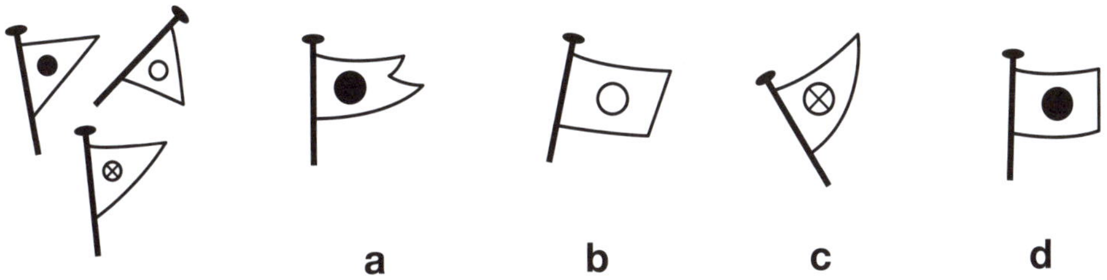

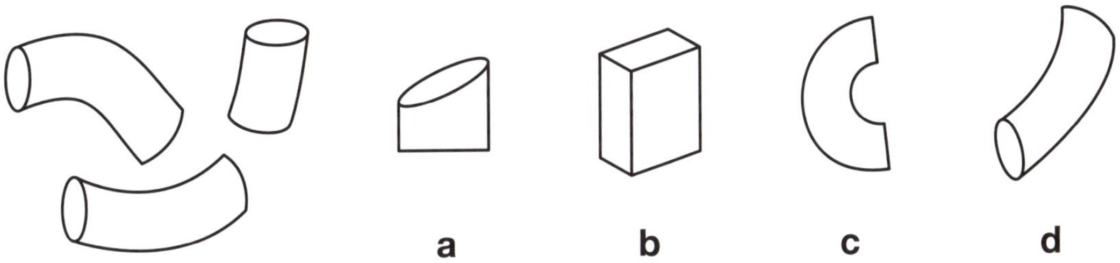

2.   a   b   c   d

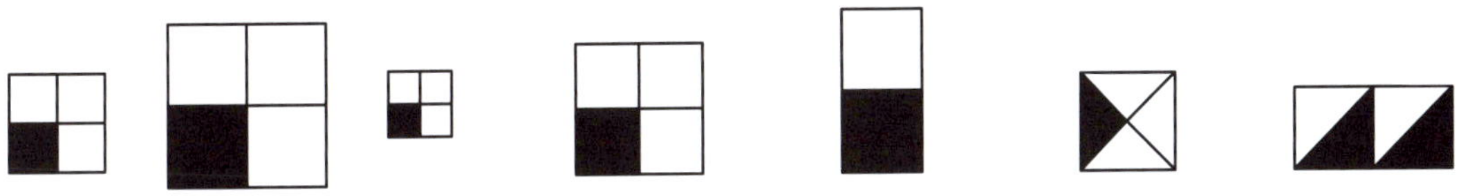

3.   a   b   c   d

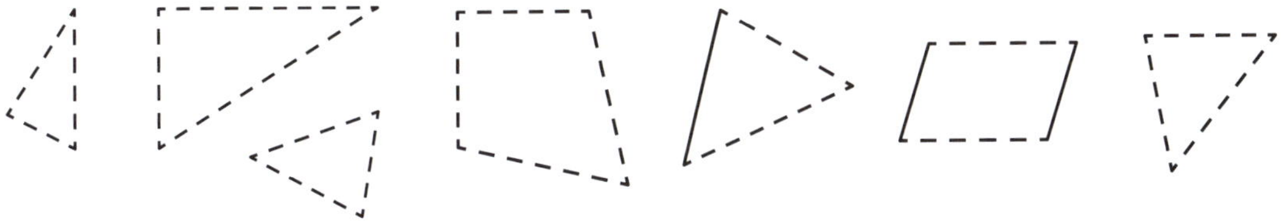

4.   a   b   c   d

5.   a   b   c   d

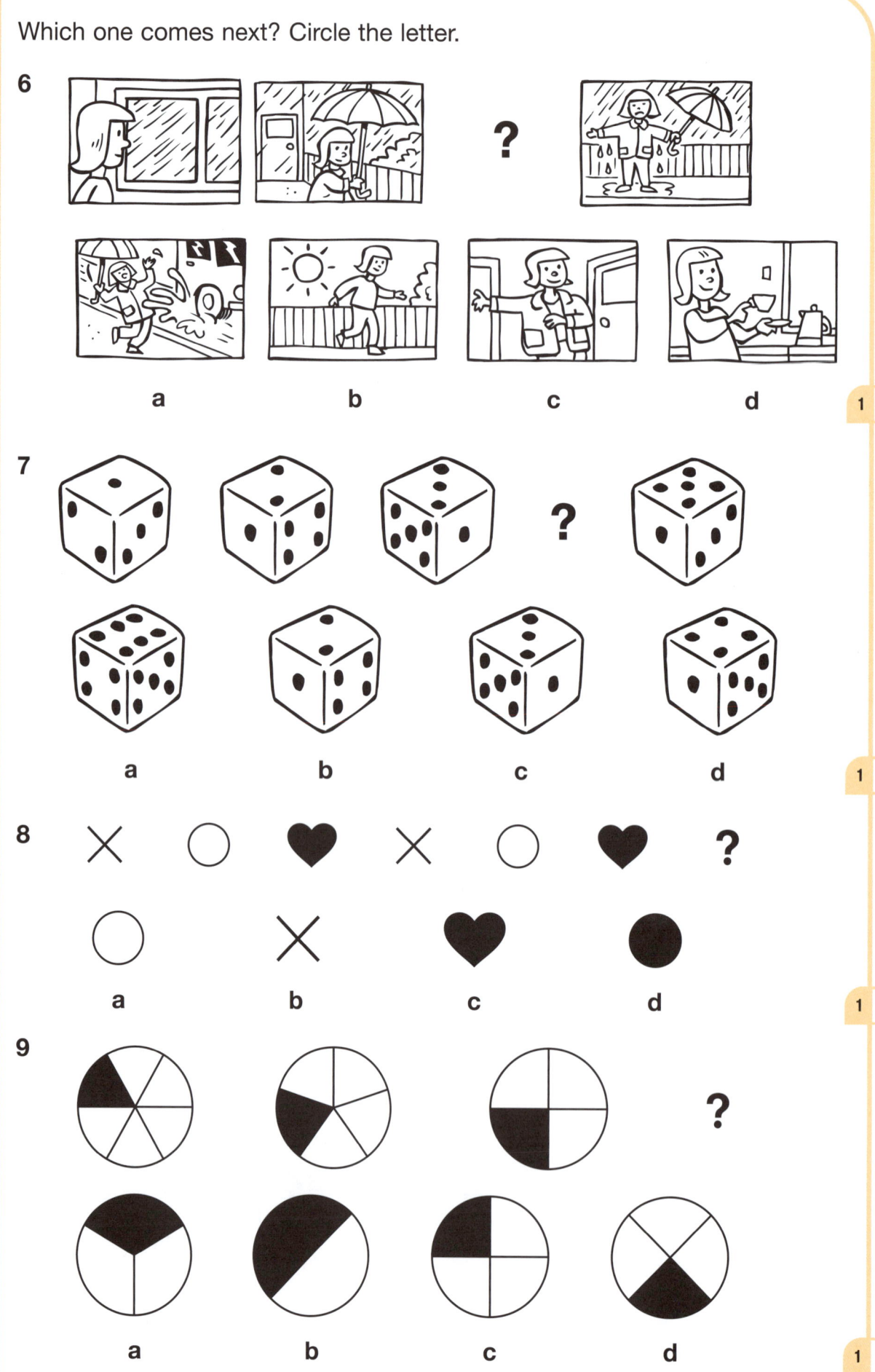

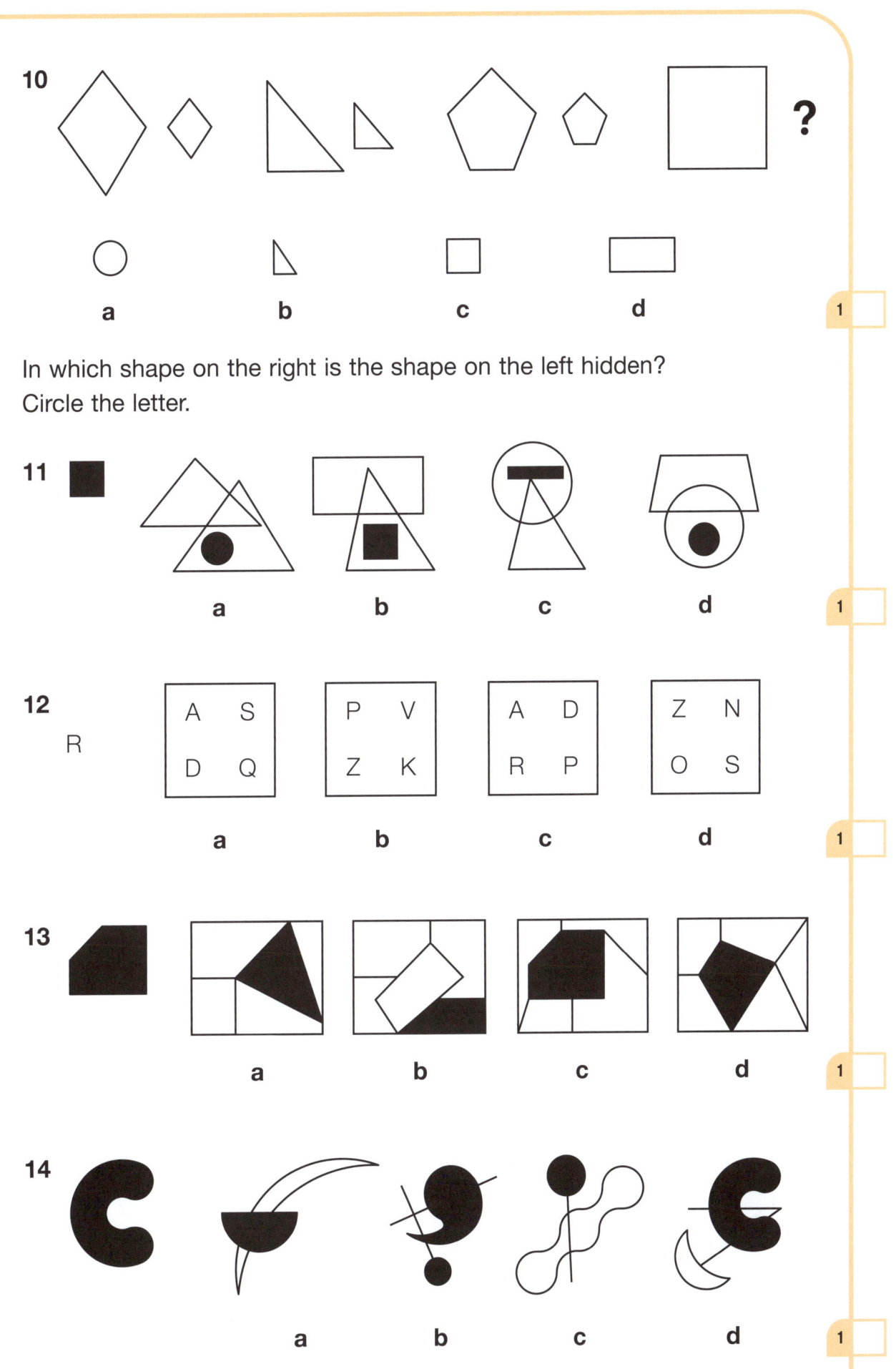

15

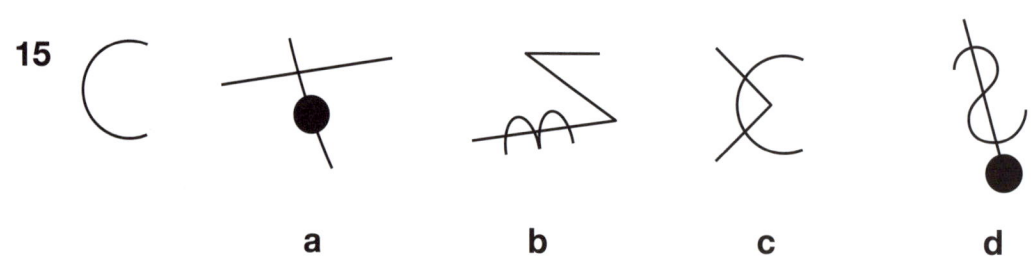

Which one completes the second pair in the same way as the first pair? Circle the letter.

16 music notes is to sheet music as scattered letters is to ?

a picture frame b tissue box c word book d globe

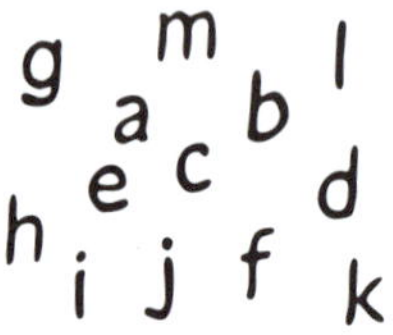

17 paw is to lion as bird foot is to ?

a cat b snake c leaf d bird

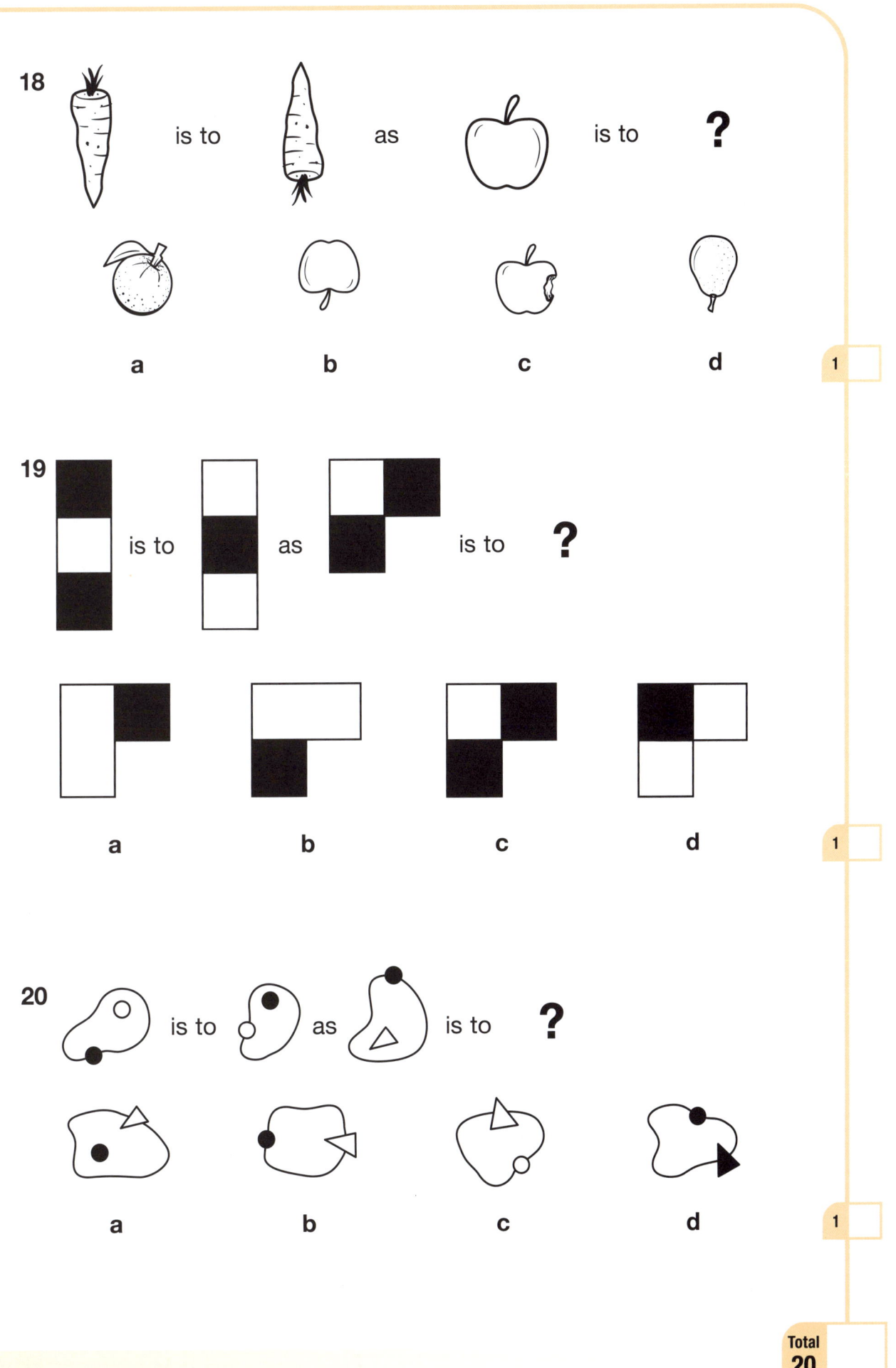

Mixed Paper 8

Which one comes next? Circle the letter.

1  ?

    a   b   c   d

2 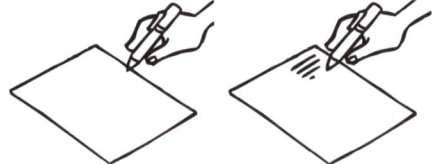 ?

    a   b   c   d

3

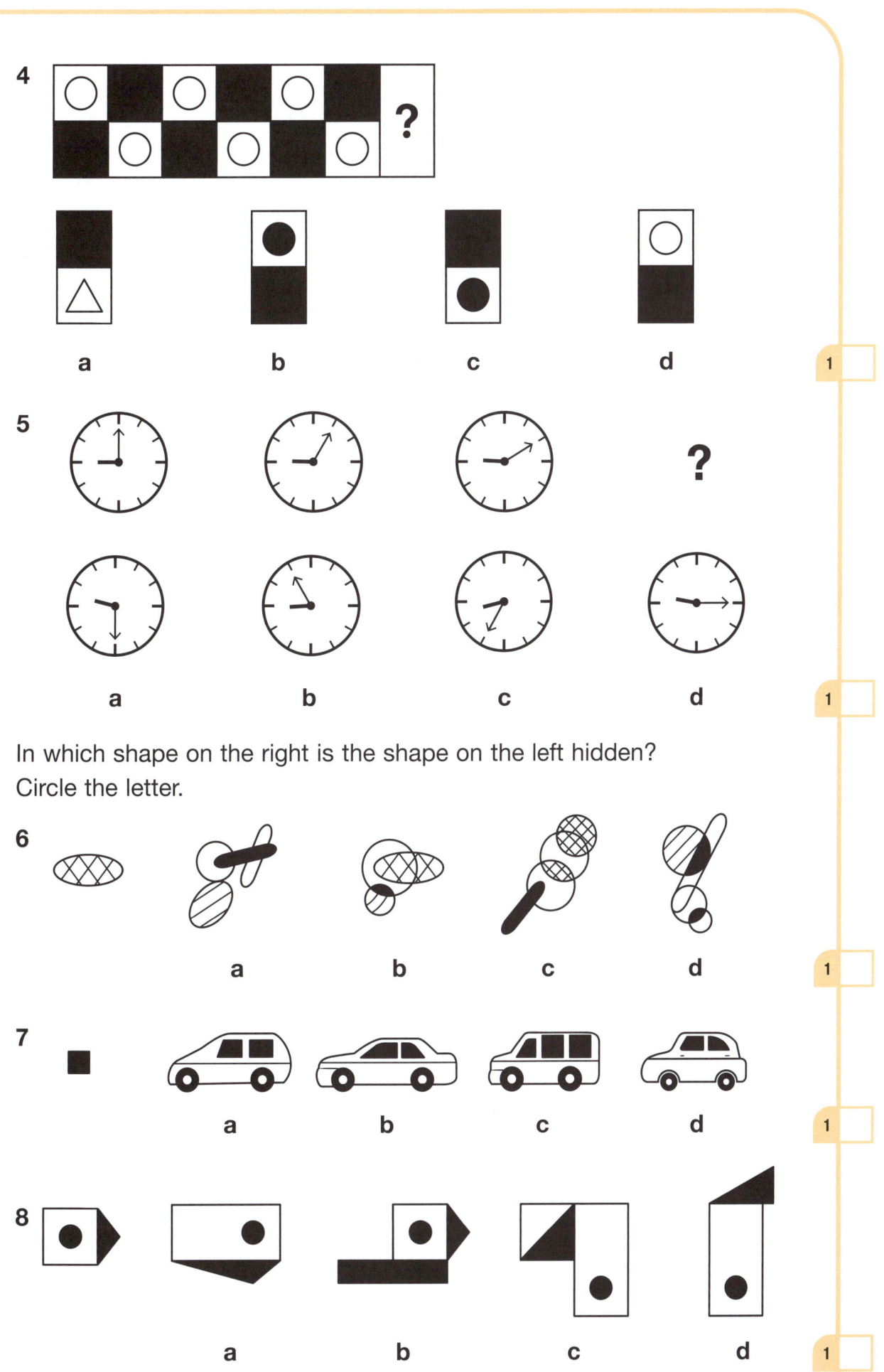

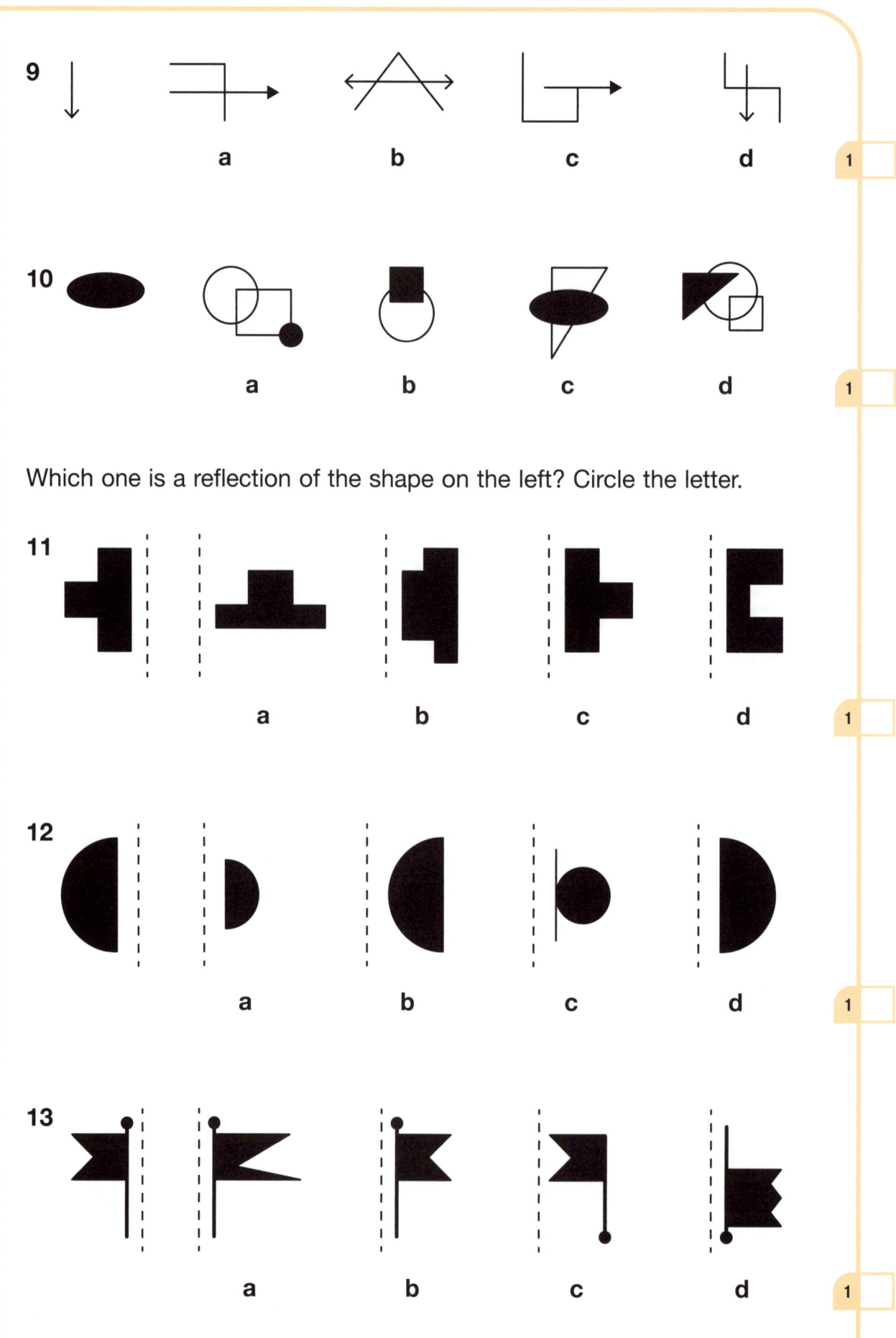

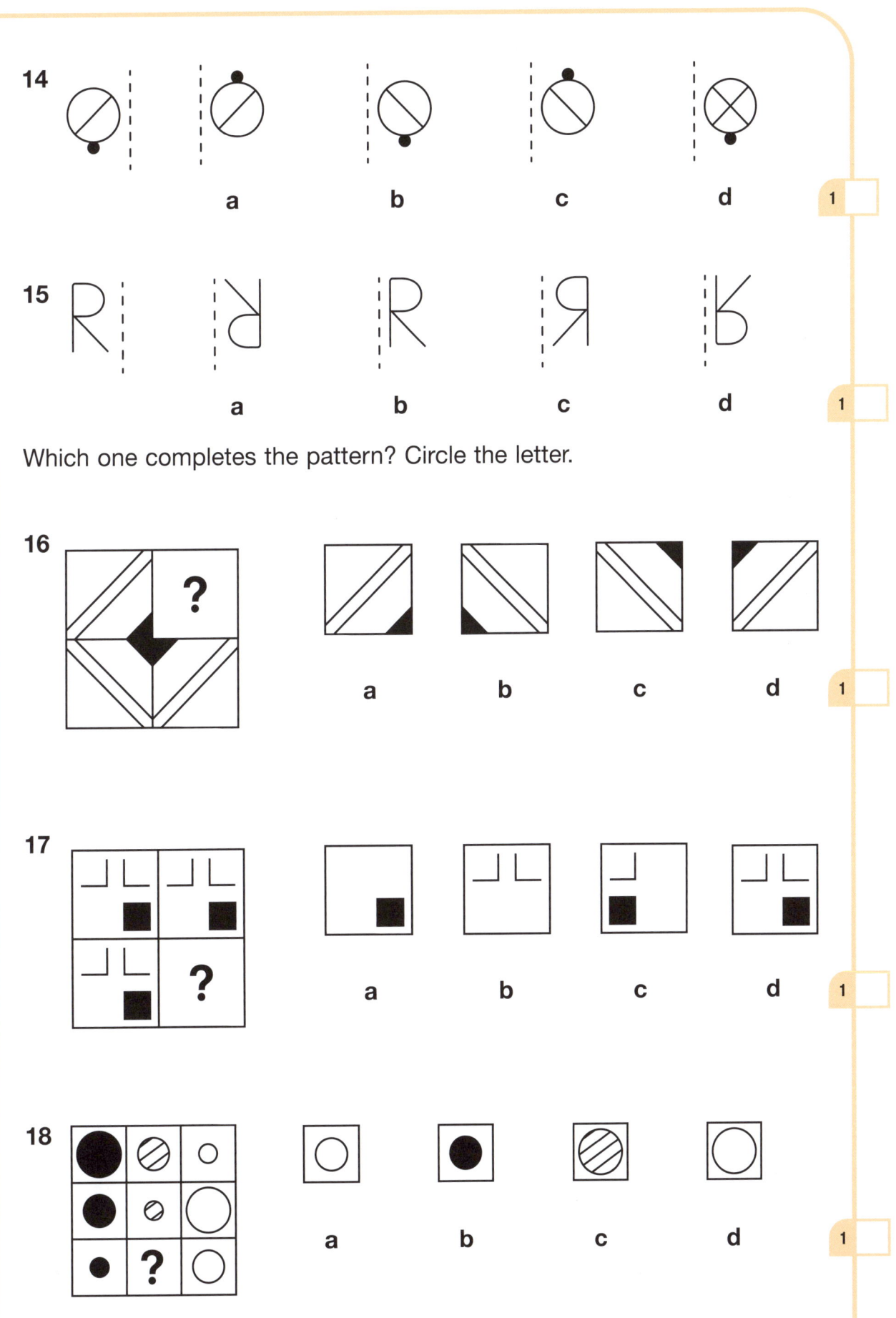

19

20

Puzzle 2

1

Complete the grid by copying the pattern in the top left quarter of the grid into each of the other quarters. Each quarter should be identical.

2

Complete the grid by reflecting the pattern in the top left quarter into each of the other quarters of the grid. The bold lines crossing the grid will be acting as mirror lines or lines of reflection.

Keywords

Some special words are used in this book. You will find them in bold the first time they appear in the Papers. These words are explained here.

horizontal	straight across
identify	to recognize a person or thing as being who or what they are
option	something chosen or that may be chosen
reflection	the result of reflecting a shape in a given mirror line
vertical	straight up or down
SPANSS	There are six different things that can change in patterns. To make sure you do not miss any of them, remembering these six words can help.
	Shape, **P**osition, **A**ngle, **N**umber, **S**hading, **S**ize. The first letters of these words give SPANSS.

Notes

Notes